Speech Class for Teens

28 Speech Class Lessons Plus Handouts and Forms

Diane Windingland

Who needs this book?

- English teachers who want a once-a-week, year-long speech class
- Speech teachers looking to add some variety to their speech classes
- Home school co-ops wanting to offer a speech class
- After school enrichment programs
- Independent instructors offering speech classes

- And, of course, the students taking the class!

Features:

- 28 Lessons for a 30 Class Sessions
- Short Lessons (suggest 10 minutes of teaching time)
- Teaching Notes provide answers to fill-in-the-blanks
- Fun, interactive activities
- All assignment sheets included (nothing to photo copy)
- Every student speaks during every class (prepared or impromptu)
- Christian content for 2 lessons (can skip or modify, if desired)
- Tested with students in 7th-11th grades
- **Class forms available online**

Save time and enjoy your class!

Please contact me with ideas, comments and suggestions for improvement.
Diane Windingland, Diane@VirtualSpeechCoach.com

Contents

Introduction to Communication and Speech...1

How this book is organized:...1

Additional supplies needed:...2

Typical Class Format...3

Grading Policy (sample)...4

Lesson 1: Introduction to Communication and Speech...5

Activity: Mute Line Up...5

Activity: Name Game..5

Activity: Name Ball (or Name Noodles!)..6

Activity: Getting to Know You Interviews...7

Successfully Speaking!...8

Class Syllabus and Materials Review..9

Lesson 2: Evaluate to Motivate..11

Lesson 3: Organizing a speech...13

Sample Speech Outline..14

Lesson 4: Ways to Start (and End) a Speech..15

Lesson 5: Effective Eye Contact—The Keyword Method...17

Activity: Speaking from Keywords..19

Lesson 6: Vocal Variety..23

Lesson 7 Your Body Speaks: Body Language and Props...25

Interpersonal Communication: Be NOSE-y..25

Why use props?...26

Lesson 8: Using Storytelling to Craft Compelling Presentations..27

Your Turn! Tell Your Story...28

Lesson 9: Research Your Topic...29

Lesson 10: Influence and Persuasion...31

Lesson 11: Conflict Resolution...33

Conflict Resolution Scenarios..34

Lesson 12: Basic Humor Tips for Public Speaking..37

Humor Tool: Self-Deprecating Humor..38

Lesson 13: Tell Your Testimony!..39

Lesson 14: Skits and Readers Theater..41

Roman's Road to the Vault Skit..42

Lesson 15: Improv Games..49

Review 51

Lesson 16: Rhetorical Devices 53

Lesson 17: Interpretive Reading 55

    Interpretive Reading Activity: The Scorpion and the Frog 56

Lesson 18: Using Dialogue 59

Lesson 19: Introducing a Speaker 61

Lesson 20: The Memorized Historical Speech 63

    How to Memorize a Speech Word for Word 64

Lesson 21: Memorable Speeches Start with Strategic Structure 65

Lesson 22: Dining Etiquette and Conversation 67

Lesson 23: Brainstorming! 69

    Solve a Problem/Offer a Solution Speech 70

Lesson 24 Group Problem Solving and Consensus 71

Lesson 25: The Panel Discussion 73

Lesson 26: Selling a Product or Service 75

Lesson 27: Job Interviewing Tips—You are selling YOU! 77

    Interview Scenarios 78

Lesson 28: Introduction to Debate 83

Appendix 1: Lesson Notes 91

Appendix 2: The Marshmallow Challenge 97

Appendix 3: Agendas 99

Appendix 4: Assignment Sheets 131

    Speaker Assignment 131

    Evaluator Assignment 147

    Impromptu Leader Assignment 154

    Grammarian Assignment 163

    Timer Assignment 169

Appendix 5: Assignment Schedules 175

    Sample 175

    Semester 1 Fill-in-the-blanks 177

    Semester 2 Fill-in-the-blanks 179

    Blank assignment sheet 181

Introduction to Communication and Speech

In numerous studies of CEO's and employers, the ability to communicate is cited as the number one job skill. In Introduction to Communication and Speech, students will develop this critical skill by learning to organize their thoughts in prepared and impromptu presentations, by using effective delivery techniques (eye contact, body language, vocal variety) and by practicing interpersonal communication skills.

This book is designed for a year-long, once a week, 30-week class of 7-20, 6th-12th grade students. There are 28 lessons. Sessions 29 and 30 are modified debates with no additional lessons. Most lessons can be taught in about 10 minutes (or combined with the warm up). The focus is on the students' oral communication. The goal is that every student will speak at every class, half of the students giving prepared speeches (14 speeches total) and the other half being evaluators, impromptu speakers and having other duties (time keeper, Ah-counter/grammarian, and impromptu leader). Two lessons have a Christian emphasis (lessons 13 and 14).

Speeches pertaining to the lesson topic are typically given in the two weeks following the lesson. The topic of the speech is generally of the student's choosing. For example, Speech #2 is Organize your Speech. That doesn't mean the topic is on organizing a speech. The topic can be on just about anything, but the skill focus is on speech organization.

The length of the speeches, the evaluations and the impromptu speeches can be adjusted to meet the time requirements of the class and the number of students. For larger classes, classes of an hour or less in length or classes of fewer than 30 sessions the number of lessons and speeches can be reduced.

How this book is organized:

Following this introduction are **a typical class format and a grading policy.**

The twenty-eight lessons follow, with a short, optional review after lesson 15.

Appendix 1: Lesson notes (with answers to fill-in-the blanks). A must-read for teachers!

Appendix 2: The Marshmallow Challenge (a fun activity for the first class of the 2nd semester)

Appendix 3:   Fill-in-the blank agendas. After a short, optional warm-up activity at the start of each class, have the students fill in the agenda for the class based on the assignment schedule for the day.

Appendix 4: Assignment sheets (Speaker, Evaluator, Impromptu Leader, Grammarian, Timer)

Note: Speakers must turn in their books at the start of class so that instructor can see the speaker's checklist. The outline for the speech must also be turned in, tucked into the book at the same place as the checklist.

Appendix 5: Assignment schedules: one sample filled out, two fill-in the blank schedules (one per semester) and one blank schedule. You can fill-in the blanks, or use your own system (your own spreadsheet), if you prefer.

> **Agendas, assignment sheets and schedule forms are available online:**
> **See the link on the first page of each form in appendices 3, 4 and 5**

Additional supplies needed:

— Timing device and a way to indicate time segments (red, yellow, and green folders, for example).

— Ah-Counter/Grammarian noise-maker for when someone uses a filler word (taping the table with a pen works)

— Tape (to tape up the word of the day)

— 50 index cards/student for speaking notes

— Extra pens and paper

— Optional: white board, markers, eraser. Instructor and students can use this, if available.

— Optional: Lectern

——Additional supplies may be needed for warm up activities and some lessons

Typical Class Format

- Warm-up Activity
- Agenda review
- Prepared Speeches
- Oral Evaluations
- Impromptu Speaking
- Lesson
- Class assignments for the next week (everyone will have an assignment):
    - Speakers*
    - Grammarian*
        - Word of the day
    - Impromptu Leader*
        - Theme
    - Evaluators
    - Timer
    - Impromptu participants

Speakers*: Students will present speeches as assigned. Typically, the subject is of the student's choosing, and may reflect a student's beliefs and values. However, all subjects and language used are to be respectful. The amount of preparation time may vary considerably from one week to the next, but students can expect to spend 1-2 hours in preparation. Preparation usually will include: brainstorming, research, organization of ideas, writing the speech, editing the speech, reducing the speech to keywords, practicing the speech, getting feedback from at least one other person, revising the speech, and practicing again at least a couple more times.

Impromptu Leader*: Prior to class, the Impromptu Leader will do 3 things: select a theme, prepare questions related to the theme and prepare a 1-2 minute talk to introduce the theme. During class, after introducing the theme, the Impromptu Leader will state a question and then call randomly on impromptu participants to respond for 1-2 minutes. Each impromptu participant should have a different question. Call on students not giving speeches in larger classes.

Grammarian*: Prior to class, the grammarian picks a word of the day for people to try to use in their presentations. The grammarian should prepare by writing out 3 things: 1. the word of the day written in large letters on a paper (which will be placed so that speakers can see it during class), 2. the definition (to read aloud during class) and 3. an original sample sentence or two, also to be read in class.

Evaluators: No preparation required prior to class. During class, evaluators will listen and watch their assigned speaker carefully, outlining the speech. There will be one minute of silence after each speaker to give the evaluators time to work on their evaluation notes. After all prepared speeches, the evaluators will present their 1-2 minute evaluations in turn.

Timer: No preparation required prior to class. During class the timer will time the following using a stop watch or other device: prepared speeches, evaluations and impromptu participants. During each of the timed presentations, the timer will hold up green, yellow and red folders to give the speaker an indication of his or her time.

*Assignment requires homework

Grading Policy (sample)

Grading Policy, 15 week semester

Grading scale (860 points possible)

90-100%	A
80-89%	B
70-79%	C
60-69%	D
< 60%	F

Points are earned in every class session, either by giving a speech (approximately every other week) or by other class participation.

7 Speeches, 100 points each = 700 points possible

General Speech Evaluation Criteria:

20	Speech assignment sheet/checklist complete and turned in
10	Outline turned in
	(Content/Delivery):
10	Related subject to audience
30	Organization (opening, body, conclusion)

- Attention-getting opening
- Support of points
- Strong conclusion and summary

30	Effective Delivery (eye contact, vocal variety, body language)

8 non-speech Class participation days, 20 points each = 160 points possible

(Participation roles include: Impromptu Leader, Impromptu Participant, Timer, Grammarian, Evaluator)

Evaluation Criteria: 0—did not do at all; 10—partial; 20—met requirements

Make-up Policy:

Non-speech Class participation cannot be made-up (each non-speech week is worth 20 points)

Speeches:

--If you know in advance that your student will miss a class, please notify me prior to the start of the semester and I will not schedule your student for that day.

--One speech may be rescheduled after the start of the semester

--speeches may also be sent via video, if rescheduling is not possible

Lesson 1: Introduction to Communication and Speech

Activity: Mute Line Up

In this simple activity the students are to line up by date of birth from youngest to oldest without talking, writing or using calendars.

Activity: Name Game

Each person takes turns stating their name, preceded by an alliterative adjective (a descriptive word that starts with the same letter as the person's first name). For example, I might introduce myself as "Dynamic Diane." The next person then says something like "Hello, Dynamic Diane! I'm Terrific Tom." The third person then adds onto the list, saying, "Hello, Dynamic Diane and Terrific Tom, I'm Jolly Julia."

AFTER playing the name game, test yourself by writing down all of the student names, with their alliterative adjective:

Alliterative adjective   Name

1. _____   _____

2. _____   _____

3. _____   _____

4. _____   _____

5. _____   _____

6. _____   _____

7. _____   _____

8. _____   _____

9. _____   _____

10. _____ _____

11. _____ _____

12. _____ _____

13. _____ _____

14. _____ _____

15. _____ _____

16. _____ _____

17. _____ _____

18. _____ _____

19. _____ _____

20. _____ _____

Activity: Name Ball (or Name Noodles!)

Actually, you can use anything that can be safely thrown, even a package of Ramen Noodles.

In this quick review of names, students throw an item to other students in the room by first saying the student's name and then throwing the item. Continue around the room until every student has caught the item.

Activity: Getting to Know You Interviews

Students will count off 1-2-3, etc.

The odd numbered students will interview the next highest even numbered student. Then the even numbered students will interview the next highest odd numbered student, with the last student interviewing student number 1. If there are an odd number of students, the teacher will participate as the last even numbered "student."

Following the interviews, the students introduce each other, starting with number 1 introducing number 2 and then number 2 introducing number 3 and so on until the last student introduces number 1.

Example with 7 students:
Because there are 7 students, the teacher will participate as #8.

First round of interviews (2-3 minutes)   Second round of interviews (2-3 minutes)
#1 interviews #2   #2 interviews #3
#3 interviews #4   #4 interviews #5
#5 interviews #6   #6 interviews #7
#7 interviews #8   #8 interviews #1

Allow 1-2 minutes to compose introductions. OK to ask questions!

Introductions: #1 introduces #2, #2 introduces #3, #3 introduces #4 and so on until #8 introduces #1.
1-2 minutes per introduction.

Name:

Age:

Family (brothers, sisters, pets):

Favorite fun activities:

What are you especially good at?

What would you like to learn?

What is something that people probably don't know about you?

Successfully Speaking!
(Reminder to teachers: answers are in Appendix 1)

Every speech has 3 main aspects:

1. _____
2. _____
3. _____

Purpose includes:

1. Your general purpose:
   a. To inform
   b. To persuade
   c. To entertain
   d. To inspire

2. Your specific purpose—your _____. Be able to write
your message in one sentence: *I will explain the basic elements of a good speech.*

3. Your desired audience outcome. Determine what you want your
audience to _____, _____, or _____. *I want the students to think
that giving a good speech is just like giving a beautifully wrapped, important gift.*

Content includes:

Organization—Introduction/Body/Conclusion
Support Material—Stories, facts, examples, memorable images
Language use—Good speeches start with good writing!
                    Write out your speech _____ _____ _____.

Delivery includes:

Eye-contact—talk to _____ not _____.
Gestures
Body Language
Appearance
Vocal Variety
Props
Enthusiasm/conviction

The best speaking advice I've ever received:

_____.

Class Syllabus and Materials Review

Class overview
- ✓ Typical Class Format
- ✓ Class materials
- ✓ Class expectations/grading
- ✓ Class agendas
- ✓ Class assignments
- ✓ Class assignment list

Questions?

Review next week's assignments

Speakers—your first speech is an icebreaker speech—it's all about you!
Tell us something interesting about yourself to help us get to know you.

Lesson 2: Evaluate to Motivate

Before the speech:
- ✓ Talk with the speaker about any specific goals for personal growth

During the speech
- ✓ Listen and watch the speaker carefully, observe audience reaction
- ✓ Take notes—on a separate piece of paper if possible

Good speeches have **POP**—Good **P**resentation, **O**rganization and a **P**urpose

POP Format

Presentation (Delivery)

+	-

Physical appearance
Manner (confident, enthusiastic)
Vocal variety, Pacing
Vocabulary
Eye contact
Any distracting mannerisms
Use of gestures
Use of props

Outline

Organization (Structure)

+	-

Clear beginning, middle, end
Opening grabs attention
Body
   A few main points
   Good transitions
Close—strong (summary, call for action)

Purpose (impact/content)

+	-

Use of humor
Use of Examples/Anecdotes
Did speaker achieve objective?
   (inform, persuade, entertain, motivate)
Appropriate to occasion, audience?

After the Speech
- ✓ Pick no more than 2-3 items to comment on in each of the POP areas, <u>organizing your comments to sandwich areas for improvement between encouraging comments about the speaker's strengths.</u> Positive/Negative (improvement)/Positive
- ✓ Compose opening and closing statements

Lesson 3: Organizing a speech

1. **Know your audience and your purpose**. (Inform?, Persuade? Entertain? Inspire?)

2. **Know your message.** Write it in one sentence (OK to change later)

3. **Brainstorm, Part 1—Idea collection** (5 minutes): Write down ideas quickly related to your topic, order does not matter.

4. **Brainstorm, Part 2—Preliminary research** (if needed, 20-30 minutes): Use outside resources (internet/books) to collect and write down more possible ideas.

5. **Idea grouping** (5 minutes): on the idea collection sheets, group related ideas using different colored highlighters or different symbols.

6. **Mind Map** using your idea collection sheets, with your main topic in the center. Use color, pictures, and lots of space. Show connections. Example:

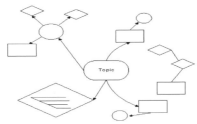

7. **Pick your best points**, given the time you have to speak, your audience and your purpose.

8. **Do more research**, if needed.

9. **Write Speech Outline**
    a. Opening—get audience's attention and lead into topic
    b. Body—Each point must be related to topic and supported
    c. Conclusion—review and end with a call to action or memorable statement. Tie into your opening, if possible (complete the circle)

    In addition to organizing by topic, you can organize chronologically, cause/effect, compare/contrast, problem/solution.

    Support your points with facts, stories, memorable images, use of props, visual aids
    Some ways to begin (and end a speech): quotes, stories, attention-getting statements

10. **Write out your speech word-for-word, but remember to write for "the ear."** Use short sentences and simple language. Pay attention to transitions between sections.

11. **Reduce to key-word notes.** Practice from key-words. DO NOT READ YOUR SPEECH.
    ## Talk to People Not Paper!

Sample Speech Outline
Actual Student outline provided by Tyler Sinclair

Topic: High school student employment

I.   Introduction
      A. Teaches responsibility
      B. Teaches real life skills
      C. Teaches how to budget

II.   Teaches responsibility
      A. Have to show up on time
      B. Have to comply with rules and procedures
      C. Have to work diligently

III. Teaches real life skills
      A. Computer/cash register skills
      B. Communication skills
      C. Job skills

IV.   Teaches how to budget money
      A. Teaches how to save
      B. Teaches how to spend money wisely
      C. Teaches about taxes

V.   Conclusion
      A. Restate 3 supports
      B. Concluding statement

Introduction:
1. Get the audience's attention
2. Give them a reason to listen
3. Preview your points
4. Transition to body

Body:
Support your points with facts, stories, examples and visual aids

Conclusion:
Review your points (don't add new points) and end with a call to action or a memorable statement

Ways to begin and end your speech:
✓ Questions
✓ Startling statements
✓ Quote/poem
✓ Story
✓ Relevant humor

Lesson 4: Ways to Start (and End) a Speech

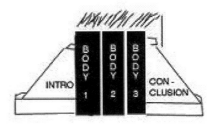

People remember best how you start and how you end!

Open your speech to grab your audience's attention and tease them so they want to hear more!

Introductions typically have 3 parts:
1. Opening
2. A hook--Speech tease or preview (your audience wants to know WIIFM? WIIFM = What's In It For Me)
3. Transition to point 1

5 Types of Speech openings/closings:
1. Ask a thought-provoking _____
2. Make a startling _____
3. Use a quote/_____
4. Tell a _____
5. Tell a relevant _____

Don't apologize, ramble or ask a trite question!

Memorize and practice your opening and closing statements

Your conclusion should summarize your main ideas and end with a bang!

In addition to the 5 openings/closings above, here are a couple of other closings:

_____ (tie the end of the speech to the beginning)

_____ ___ _____

Lesson 5: Effective Eye Contact—The Keyword Method

Step 1: Write out your speech. Pay careful attention to the introduction, the conclusion and the transitions. Here's a nifty trick to help you trigger your memory as you transition to different parts of your speech: use the same word or phrase from the end of one sentence to the beginning of another as you transition. For example: *"There are only 3 things we have to fear: 1. Bad men, 2. Bad decisions and 3. Bad breath. Bad breath is a bigger problem than you might think . . ."* The phrase "bad breath" triggers my memory for the next sentence.

Step 2: Practice it a few times, revising it as necessary.

Step 3: Write out key words and phrases. You can also draw pictures/symbols. Try not to have more than 4-5 words per sentence or per line. Use a big font if typing. Double space.

It might look something like this:

> Beginning, women, survival, groceries
>
> Men, hunters, women, gatherers
>
> Today, woman, primary, sex-linked
>
> Story: daughter, license, Target

Step 4: Set your written speech aside and practice from the keywords (OK to look back at first, but then resist the urge). Practice your introduction and conclusion so that you can at least do those from memory—those are the parts people will remember the most.

You don't have to say your speech the same way twice—No one will know if you use different words!

In fact, by allowing yourself the freedom to deviate from what you've written, you are less likely to "blank out" if your mind can't think of the one exact phrase you had written.

Giving the speech

The MAIN THING to remember is: **Speak to People, Not Paper!** Don't look at your notes and have your mouth moving at the same time. Eye contact while speaking is important for audience engagement. Look down. Grab a few key words on a line. Look up. Speak. Repeat.

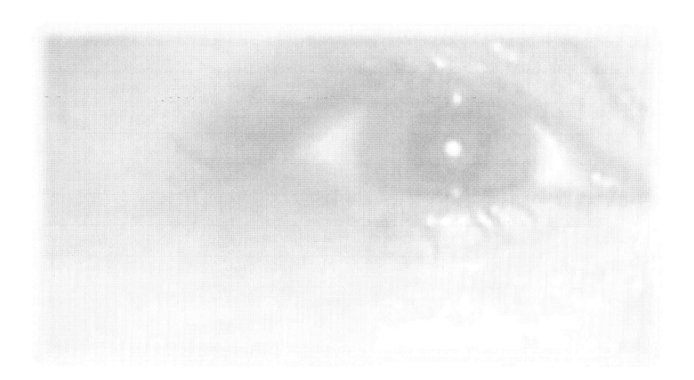

Activity: Speaking from Keywords

The Effects of Music on Plants*

Music can have a profound effect on all living things. Of course, we know that different music can make a person feel sad or happy, relaxed, energetic or even irritated. But new scientific evidence shows that certain types of music can actually affect plants and animals. In an experiment done with petunias, bean and corn, three groups of plants were given three different auditory environments. Soil, water and light levels were controlled and the same for each. It was found that plants growing in boxes with music by Mozart, Vivaldi and Bach grew taller, faster and produced more fruit than the plants with no music. However, the most amazing thing is that the plants continuously exposed to rock music were smaller and actually began to slant away from the source of the sound. After six weeks of continuous exposure to loud rock music radio, many of the plants died.

*exercise from Institute for Excellence in Writing class

The Effects of Music on Plants

1._____

2._____

3._____

4._____

5._____

6._____

7._____

8._____

Lesson 6: Vocal Variety

Characteristics of a Good Voice

Quality—Your voice should convey friendliness and be _____ to listen to.

Volume—Control the volume. Don't shout at your audience, but speak loudly enough to be heard.

   "Talk from your _____ _____"

Pitch—Vary your pitch. Don't be _____.

Rate—Number of words per minute (WPM).

   A good rate is typically 125-160 WPM

Figure your WPM:

Read a paragraph out loud at a conversational rate. Time yourself from start to finish. Count the number of words (or use the word count feature of MS Word).

WPM = (# Words/time in seconds) X 60.

Example:

When I read the paragraph from lesson 5, which has 149 words, I timed myself reading for 1:11 min.

1:11 on the stop watch is 71 seconds
(149 words/71 seconds) X 60 seconds/min= 126 WPM

Do this a couple more times and average your WPM. You can use your WPM to figure out how approximately how many words long your speeches need to be

Time allowed for speech X WPM = Approx. Number of Words long for your speech.

Using my example, if I want to give a 10 minute speech and I want to know about how many works long to make it: 10 minutes X 126 WPM = 1260 words. I can easily check my word count on MS Word (review tab)

> **Your turn:** If it takes you 1:40 to read something with 200 words, what is your WPM? About how many words would you need for a 5 minute speech?

Emphasis can change meaning!

I did not say you stole my red hat.

I **did** not say you stole my red hat.

I did **not** say you stole my red hat.

I did not **say** you stole my red hat.

I did not say **you** stole my red hat.

I did not say you **stole** my red hat.

I did not say you stole **my** red hat.

I did not say you stole my **red** hat.

I did not say you stole my red **hat.**

Lesson 7 Your Body Speaks: Body Language and Props

Interpersonal Communication: Be NOSE-y

N _____

O _____   _____   _____

S _____

E ____   _____

 A "Secret" method: Mirroring

Body Language and Gestures in a Presentation:

- Stand Tall—"String theory"
- Use NOSE in speeches, too!
- Mirror the energy level of your audience at first
- Don't move all the time
    - —it's OK to stand still or have your hands at your side
- Use open hands (don't point with one finger)
- Use gestures for
    - Size, weight, shape, direction and location
    - Importance or urgency
    - Comparison and Contrast
- More advanced:
    - Staging—position yourself for a scene, timeline, or points
    - Bigger gestures for bigger audiences

Props and Visual Aids:

- Reinforce your point
- Enhance understanding or remembrance
- Save time
- Display just before you are ready to use
- Look at people not props or visual aids
- Practice, practice, _____!

Why use props?

- Make your presentation more memorable (visuals are more easily remembered)
- Explain, demonstrate or illustrate a concept
- Show what you are talking about
- Add humor
- Add variety (get and keep attention)
- Use to get into "character"

What are props?

- Objects
- Video/Audio: DVD/Video/CD/mp3
- Posters/Pictures/Graphs/Charts
- Whiteboard/Flip Charts
- PowerPoint
- Handouts

Consider using a prop as a metaphor (stands for something else).

Examples:

- A magnifying glass to illustrate focus or searching
- An easily bendable soda straw to symbolize being flexible.
- An extra bouncy ball to symbolize resiliency and bouncing back from difficult situations.
- A rope made up of many strands (each strand by itself is weak but together they are strong)
- A mirror (look at yourself and see the greatness within)
- A star (reach for the stars or you are a star or find your star)
- A bag of marbles (don't lose all your marbles)
- Some sort of birthday paraphernalia (celebrate that today is a new beginning)
- A fake ball and chain (what is holding you back?)
- Luggage (what baggage is weighing you down?)

7 Tips on using props:

1. Do not use a prop just to use a prop. There should be a specific reason.
2. Practice using the prop.
3. Reveal only when using, if possible.
4. Less is more. Do not use too many props. Do not put too much information on a visual.
5. If relying on electronics, animals or other people carefully consider what could happen! Practice and set up early! Have a backup plan.
6. Make sure the prop is big enough to be seen by the audience. If audio is involved, make sure it is loud enough. Do a distance check.
7. Do not speak at the prop. Speak to your audience.

Lesson 8: Using Storytelling to Craft Compelling Presentations

Why tell stories?

1. People _____ stories.
   If people remember your stories they will remember your message!

   a. Stories tap into _____.

   b. Stories are _____.

   Statistics are abstract. Stories give meaning and relevance.

2. Stories _____ you to your listener.
   a. Common ground—I'm like you.
   b. Integrity/values—I'm a good person. You can trust me.
   c. Vulnerability—I trust you enough to tell you this.

3. As a presenter, or in conversation, stories are easy to _____.

How to craft a story:

1. **Know what you want to accomplish.** What do you want your audience to feel, think, and do?
2. **Know your point.** No pointless stories!
3. **Know your audience**—their viewpoints, needs, knowledge, etc.
4. **Paint a picture**—describe setting and character vividly. Use dialog.
5. **Get them in the gut**—connect with emotions
6. **Uncover the humor**—in essence humor occurs with surprise/contradiction
7. **Conflict is necessary.** Your story must have a conflict/problem!
8. **Dump the parts that do not address your point.**
9. **Tell it to someone.** Practice in conversation.
10. **Refine and Repeat**

Your Turn! Tell Your Story

1. Want to accomplish: _____

2. My Point : _____

3. My audience: _____

4. Paint a picture (relevant setting information):

5. Get them in the gut (what created feelings of Joy, Sadness, Fear, Anger or Frustration):

6. Humor in the situation?

8. Story Structure: _____ (Traditional example)

   • Main character:

   • inciting event (a problem):

   • What happened leading to the climax:

   • Climax/Turning point:

   • Resolution/solution:

8. Dump what doesn't support your point
9. Tell it to someone!
10. Refine and Repeat

Lesson 9: Research Your Topic

Use the Organize your Speech process from lesson 3 to explore your topic

Decide on your general purpose: Inform, persuade, entertain, inspire

For the "Research Your Topic" Assignment, inform or persuade

Types of Support Material:
- **Statistics:** Numerical ways of conveying information about incidents, data and events
- **Facts:** Verifiable information (i.e. you didn't just make it up)
- **Testimony:** Quotes or opinions from experts
- **Examples, stories or anecdotes:** Relate events that happened to you or someone else
- **Visual Aids:** Diagrams, charts, pictures, models

How to begin: Start with what you already _____. Research the gaps.

Research Sources:
- **Search the web (my favorite!)**
  - Ask "Dr. Google" –Input key words or questions into your browser
  - You can also use Google Scholar
    - Narrow your search by being specific and using quotes around search terms
    - Save or "favorite" your sources
  - Online databases through your library
- **Library books/magazines**—Start early in case you need to request materials!
  - ask a librarian for help
  - Look at the table of contents/index/appendices for ideas and organization
- **Interview people**
- **Original research** (observation, experimentation, survey)

Combining multiple sources:
- Combine like ideas—take what is most interesting or best supports your points
  - Online (WebNotes/bookmarks), files/folders on your computer, notebook, index cards, post-it notes, highlighting, mind-mapping

- Keep track! Number your sources and write the number next to the excerpt

Keep asking—does this support my main point? If not, throw it out!

Lesson 10: Influence and Persuasion

7 Fundamental Motivators

Scarcity going, going . . .

Social Proof—peer _____

C_____ I said I would

C_____ This is how I am/what I believe

Reciprocity others do unto you as you have done unto them

Authority someone people respect/believe

Likeability I like you

12 Most Persuasive Words in the English Language

According to a Yale University study, the twelve most persuasive words are:

You	Money	Save	New
Results	Easy	Health	Safety
Love	Discovery	Proven	Guarantee

You is #1

Use this knowledge to "Look at All, Speak to One" in presentations

Instead of:		Use:
Have any of you . . .	→	Have you . . .
Everyone in here has a special gift . . .	→	You have a special gift . . .

Monroe's Motivated Sequence—for the persuasive speech!

1. **Attention**: Hey! Listen to me, you have a PROBLEM!
2. **Need**: Let me EXPLAIN the problem.
3. **Satisfy**: But, I have a SOLUTION!
4. **Visualization**: If we IMPLEMENT my solution, this is what will happen. Or, if we don't implement my solution, this is what will happen.
5. **Action**: You can help me in this specific way. Can you help me?
6. **Rebuttal**: Other people may say this, but MY solution is best.

Lesson 11: Conflict Resolution

Or, How to Deal with People Who Drive You Crazy!

Your top "crazy-makers:"

Person: _____
situation:_____

Person: _____
situation:_____

What is your usual response to conflict?

Fight _____

Flight _____

Freeze _____

Face _____

Build your relationships . . . LEAP into Conflict Resolution!

Apply to one of your "Crazy-maker" situation:

Listen Reflectively: _____

Empathize: _____

Agree
  On the problem: _____
  On common ground: _____

Partner: _____

33

Conflict Resolution Scenarios

Scenario 1 (2 girls): Mom and teenage daughter at the dinner table (give cell phone to teen girl):

Mom: *Please don't use your cell phone at the dinner table, _____.*

Daughter: . . . . (ignore "mom" don't even look up)

Mom (loudly, yelling): *Turn off your cell phone this minute or else!*

Daughter: *Oh, leave me alone!*

Mom: *You're so selfish!*
If you don't turn it off now, I'll rip it out of your hands!

Daughter: *pfft. . . You don't want me to have any friends. I hate you!*

Scenario 2 (2 boys): soccer team mates coming home from a losing game, sitting in Boy 2's brand new car, Boy 1 has just spilled a bottle of Mountain Dew

Boy 1: *Oh, man. . .I'm sorry!*

Boy 2: (driving, looks down briefly)
My new car! You spilled pop in my new car!
How can you be so clumsy?!
Oh, I forgot. . .you choked on the penalty kick, too. How could you miss that wide open net??. . .you are so pathetic!

Boy 1: *I'm pathetic?!? Just because you have a shiny new car doesn't mean your life is perfect! I heard that the police came by your house last week for what was it? Oh, yeah— domestic violence. . .*

Boy 2: (still driving) *Hey, Leave my family out of this. . .Loser.*
     Just shut up!

Boy 1: *Yeah. . .I'll shut up. I wouldn't want to have a battle of wits with   an unarmed person.*

Boy 2: (driving, but now turns and stares at Boy 1, who stares back) *What?? Battle of the wits? I. . .*
>>>>CRASH<<<<<< (car crash)

Scenario 3a (5 students):

As a simple example, a supervisor is dismayed about a policy change his manager just told him about. He must now meet with his very independent crew members every day instead of a couple of times a week. The other 4 volunteers are role-playing possible responses that an upper level manager might make. Feel free to adlib a bit—play it up and have fun!

Supervisor:
We have to meet with our crew members every day?? You've got to be joking! They won't want to do that!

Person #1 (Manager) Fight—
(roll eyes, disdainful attitude) *You're the one joking, right? Tell me you're not that spineless. It's really not so hard. Just tell them, "It's my way or the highway!*

(instructor briefly points out that this is an example of the fight response)

Person #2 (Manager) Flight—
(apathetic) *Well, if you don't like the new policy, take it up with the director. I'm just the messenger.*

(instructor briefly points out that this is an example of the flight response)

Person #3 (Manager) Freeze—
(Nonchalant, accommodating)

You're right. I hate it when they change the rules. I guess it's not a big deal. If what you're doing works, why change?

(instructor briefly points out that this is an example of the freeze response)

Person #4 (Manager) Face—
(friendly, empathetic) *Help me understand. Why do you think they won't want to do it?*

(instructor briefly points out that this is an example of the face response)

Applying LEAP to the previous scenario

Scenario 3b

Supervisor:
We have to meet with our crew members every day?? You've got to be joking! They won't want to do that!

Person #1 (Manager) Listen reflectively—
Help me understand. Why do you think they won't want to do it?

Supervisor: *Well, I guess it just seems like meetings are a big waste of time.*

Person #1 (Manager) clarifying—
"So, your crew will think meeting daily is a waste of time?"

Supervisor: *Yes, they will!*

Person #2 (Manager) Empathize—
I can understand how they would feel. In my last job, there were so many meetings it was hard to get any work done!

Person #3 (Manager) Agree—
So, if they saw that the meetings would help them be more productive, they'd be more likely to support the change, wouldn't they? (nod)

Supervisor—*They probably would! But they don't like being told what to do.*

Person #4 (Manager) Partner—
They probably have some ideas of their own for increasing productivity. Do you think they would like to be part of the decision-making process before we make the change?

Supervisor—*They definitely have opinions! Yeah, that would be a good idea!*

Lesson 12: Basic Humor Tips for Public Speaking

Key Point # 1:

        People laugh when their minds are successfully _____.

Key Point #2:

_____ is everything

    2a. You need to pause _____the punch line!

    2b. You need to pause _____the punch line!

Key Point #3

Rule of 3. Have 3 items in a series, the first 2 being _____(the "set up") and the 3rd causing a

_____ in direction (punch line)

I was nervous about the trip so I took a flashlight, a blanket, and. . . _____.

              (-------   Set up---------) \Pause

                                \Pause

                                >Punch line

To be a persuasive speaker you need _____, _____, and _____.

10 logical essentials:

_____

_____

10 exaggerated essentials:

_____

_____

Handout based on presentation by Darren LaCroix

Put Yourself Down to Bring the Laughter Up!

Humor Tool: Self-Deprecating Humor

"Self-deprecating humor should always be two-pronged. It should comically acknowledge a criticism or situation, but also infer that there is no substance to it and that you're in the driver's seat."-Robert Orben

Your Life as Material

Step 1. Make Lists

Negative Personality traits/shortcomings	Unique traits (esp. physical)	Things that make you angry	Things you worry about	Things that frighten you
controlling	2nd degree black belt	Losing things	Forgetting where I parked	Unprotected heights
Too task-oriented		Unaccountable people	Getting fat	Jump scenes In movies
Directionally impaired		Bad traffic when I'm in a rush	Running out of money	

Step 2 Add attitude—

Rant and rave on a topic without trying to be funny. I hate . . .
Then try to take a mocking attitude. I love . . . or I'm proud of . . .

Step 3: Apply formulas—Incongruity

Exaggeration
An unspoken truth
Set up . . . Punch line
Rule of 3's (expected, expected . . . unexpected)
Use a prop?

The author's
"Fat Booth" app picture

Lesson 13: Tell Your Testimony!

A testimony is a story that illustrates a point.
It is a *personal* story, so it has the power to help people see themselves and their own feelings in your experience.

A typical testimony has 3 parts:

BEFORE
DURING
AFTER

Using a Christian testimony as an example:

BEFORE—Give details, examples or a story of what your life was like before you had a personal relationship with Christ. What were some of your feelings and struggles? Lack of peace? Fear of death? Something missing? Lonely? Longing to be loved/accepted?

DURING—Describe the circumstances that caused you to get serious about having a personal relationship with Christ.

AFTER—Give details about how your life has changed since you accepted Christ. What are you excited about?

A Christian testimony is about what God has done *for* you and what God has done *in* you. Jesus is the star, not you.

The same format can be used for other testimonials as well (products, services, etc.)

Your Turn! Choose one: Christian Testimony or Product/Service Testimony

BEFORE (problems/struggles):

DURING (What were the circumstances of the change):

AFTER (What has changed?):

Lesson 14: Skits and Readers Theater

The Romans Road to Salvation—basis for an in-class skit

Are we on a dead-end road?

Problem: We all deserve death!

Romans 3:23

For all have sinned and fall short of the glory of God.

Romans 6:23 (1st half)

For the wages of sin is death. . .

Solution: Christ paid the price for our sins!

Romans 6:23 (2nd half)

. . .but the gift of God is eternal life in Christ Jesus our Lord.

Romans 5:8

. . .while we were still sinners, Christ died for us.

Action—What we must do.

Romans 10:9,10

If you confess with your mouth, "Jesus is Lord,"
and believe in your heart that God raised him from the dead,
you will be saved.
For it is with your heart that you believe and are justified,
 and it is with your mouth that you confess and are saved.

The Promise!

Romans 10:13

Everyone who calls on the name of the Lord will be saved.

Roman's Road to the Vault Skit
By Shane Yancey

Actors: 1 narrator, 6 gymnasts

Setting/Props: *In center stage stand the first three gymnasts, in a straight line waiting for their turn on the vault. The conversation always takes place between the first two people in line while the third person listens. As one gymnast leaves a new one comes in to take his/her place.*

1: So, are you scared?

2: No, vault is one of my best events.

1: Yea, mine too but I still get a little scared every time.

2: Well, I do get a little nervous but never scared.

1: Wow! Are you that good?

2: No not really. I just have the best coach in the world.

1: You mean you're from "Heaven's Gym"?

2: Yea. It's great there!

1: Must be nice.

2: You don't like your gym--where did you say you were from?

1: I'm from the "World's Gym"

2: Oh, I've heard that y'all don't have very good coaches over there.

1: That's an understatement; we barely have coaches at all. It's just a bunch of different guys walking around telling us all kinds of different stuff, none of which ever seems to work. It must be nice to have one coach with all the right answers. Oh, they're calling my name--I'm up.

1 runs off stage and 4 walks on. 2, 3 and 4 stand and watch 1 vault making head motions like she fell really bad.

Narrator: *Romans 3:23. " for all have sinned and fallen short of the glory of God"*

2: Wow! That must have really hurt, I have never seen anyone try to land on their hands before.

3: He wasn't trying to land on his hands. Besides he has had worse falls.

2: I've never seen any worse.

3: That's why I could never go to your gym.

2: Why is that?

3: Because I am just not good enough, I mean I could never be perfect.

2: Oh, don't get me wrong, we're not perfect! We were all as bad as that once and we all still fall but not as much and never that hard, and even when we do, our coach is always there to catch us. Our coach doesn't want perfect gymnasts. I mean if you're already perfect what do you need a coach for?

3: I guess that's true but I mean I'm really bad--your coach would never take me.

2: No--actually he would want you more, the worse the better. Think about it like this-- if you're really bad when you come to our coach, and once under him you become great think about how much better of an image other people will have of our coach. --Hey I'm up--see ya.

2 runs off and 5 walks on. 3, 4 and 5 make head motions and ooohs as 2 does a perfect vault.

Narrator *Romans 5:8 " But God demonstrates his own love for us in this: While we were still sinners, Christ died for us."*

3: Wow! His coach must be really good!

4: Yes our coach is really good!

3: Oh—he's your coach too?

4: Yes.

3: Well, he must be really good, but he sounds kind of big-headed. I mean bringing all of that glory to himself by teaching the worst kids.

4: No, no. It's not like that at all. It's not like he is big-headed and has to have all the glory. We are just so grateful; we want him to have all the glory. He does it simply because he loves us.

3: Yea, I am sure he gets something out of it.

4: Just our love, and that's really all he wants. See, he gave up a lot for us.

3: What do you mean? He is the best coach in the world. He must have everything.

4: No, he gave it all up for us. He gave up all his money and all his medals so that we would have everything we needed. Everything he ever earned or deserved, he gave up for us.

3: Yea, but at least he gets to spend every day doing gymnastics, something he loves.

4: No, not really. His body is so broken from working with us he can't even do a cartwheel.

3: But that last gymnast said he always caught you when you fell. If his body is that broken, it must really hurt him to catch you.

4: It does.

3: Then why does he do it?

4: I don't know. Hey, isn't that you they are calling?

3: Oh, yea.

3 runs off, and 6 walks on. 4 and 5 make head movements as 3 runs straight into the vaulting horse.

Narrator: Romans 6:23 "For the wages of sin is death, but the gift of God is eternal life in Christ Jesus our Lord."

4: Is he going to be OK?

5: Yea, as soon as he regains consciousness he will be fine. It happens all the time.

4: All the time? It's a miracle that he's not hurt or even dead after that fall.

5: Well, most of our gymnasts do usually have to quit because they get hurt. Actually all of us end up like that.

4: Then why do you stay with those coaches?

5: Well, it's because they're the only ones I know of.

4: Well, how about my coach? I told you he's great.

5: Yea, just another coach with another gimmick.

4: No, it is not like that at all. He really has all the right answers; I mean he practically wrote the book on gymnastics. If you train under his ways you are not only guaranteed a longer gymnastics career but one with a lot fewer injuries.

5: Well, I guess my coaches can't guarantee that.

4: Well, mine can. Oh, I'm up.

4 runs off. 5 and 6 makes head motions as 4 does a perfect vault.

Narrator: Romans 10: 9-10 " That if you confess with your mouth, 'Jesus is Lord,' and believe in your heart that God raise him from the dead, you will be saved. For it is with your heart that you believe and are justified, and it is with your mouth that you confess and are saved."

5: Wow! That was beautiful.

6: Yeah, ever since he has been training with our coach his vaults have been pretty good.

5: I consider it a good vault if I don't have to be carried off on a stretcher. Man, I wish I had your coach.

6: Well, wish no more, just come to our gym. He would love to have you.

5: Yeah, but I couldn't afford it, it must really cost a lot to have the best.

6: Haven't you been listening? He does it out of love, it won't cost you anything.

5: You mean to tell me that it's free? I don't have to do anything?

6: Well, not exactly nothing.

5: Great. Here comes the big catch. What is it my first born child or something?

6: No. Actually all you have to do is go up to him and ask-- just tell him you are a bad gymnast and need him to make it in gymnastics.

5: Just ask?

6: Yep, that's it. Then follow his direction, and do all your gymnastics like he says.

5: OK. Now I see I have to be his slave.

6: No, it is not like that. Think about it. If you know you have the coach with all the right answers that can make you one of the world's best gymnast then why wouldn't you listen to him?

5: Good point. But just one more thing, I have never seen your coach. How do I know that he is that good?

6: Well, I guess by looking at us--his students. Here comes our score now. A 9.999.

5: You mean it's not a perfect 10?

6: Hey, we'll never be perfect, but if we listen to our coach we get real close. Hey, they're calling your name.

5 starts to run off the stage opposite from all the others.

6: Hey, the vault is that way! Where are you going?

5: Now that I know the best way to be a gymnast, do you think I am going to waste one more vault doing it the wrong way? I am going to see your coach right now.

5 turns to leave then stops.

Narrator Romans 10:13 " for, everyone who calls on the name of the Lord will be saved."

5 turns back around.

5: By the way what did you say your coach's name was?

6: Just call him Jesus.

6 walks off the stage as the Narrator reads Romans 10:14.

Narrator Romans 10:14 "How, then, can they call on the one they have not believed in? And how can they believe in the one of whom they have not heard? And how can they hear without someone preaching to them?

Lesson 15: Improv Games

Improv teaches you to go with the flow and to think on your feet. It also strengthens speaking and listening skills while teaching cooperation. And, best of all, it's fun!

Some easy improv games:

1. **One word story** (3 minutes) **Lesson: Giving up control**
(give scene— ex: Walking a dog down Main Street):
Participants line up and tell a story one word at a time, until the story comes to some sort of conclusion (or it is apparent that it won't!).

2. **Yes, and. . . (Line or Circle) Lesson: working on affirming and adding instead of negating.**
The first person makes a positive, declarative statement, such as, "It was a beautiful day at the park today." The next person continues with his own, single, declarative statement that furthers the story (moves it forward) PRECEEDING it with "Yes, and. . ." For example, "Yes, and it was difficult to find a place to park the car." Continue until the story reaches a logical conclusion. .

3. **Mirror, Mirror (Partner)**
Lesson: Really paying attention to the other person
Level 1: Participants partner, with one person as #1 and the other as #2. The partners take turns mirroring each other's actions (actions are to be performed in slow motion). Also mirror emotions (facial expressions) The teacher designates which one is the leader (#1 or #2) and will "randomly" say switch (the leader becomes the follower). Level 2: Both participants follow and lead, taking turns without talking and without the teacher saying switch.

4. **Zip-Zap-Zoop (Circle)**
One of the players points to another player to one side of them and says 'zip'. That player turns to the next player in the circle, points to them and says 'zip'. Thus the 'zip' zips around the circle in one direction. At any time a receiving player can say 'zap' to the person pointing at them. When they do the player that said 'zip' and was pointing at them must change direction of the pointing. This means that they must quickly turn around, point and say 'zip to the person that just pointed at them. Now the 'zip' can zip around the circle, but changing direction every time there is a 'zap'. Lastly the person that receives the 'zip' may elect to yell 'zoop' and point at someone anywhere in the circle. That player then restarts the 'zip' going in the direction of their choice. The group must really pay attention for this to work.

5. **Slap-Clap-Snap (Circle) Lesson: Divided attention**
Participants line up and all begin rhythmically slapping their thighs, then clapping, then snapping their fingers, after which one person starts with a word (on the slap). Then at the beginning of each sequence of slap-clap-snaps, the next person in line says a word that begins with the last letter of the previous word

Review

4 speech purposes: _____, to _____, to _____, to _____

To make good eye contact, talk to _____ not _____.

Label the outline with Topic, Introduction, Conclusion, Main Points 1, 2, 3 and supporting points 1-1, 1-2, 2-1, 2-2, 3-1, 3-2.

- _____
- _____
  - ○ _____
  - ○ _____
- _____
  - ○ _____
  - ○ _____
- _____
  - ○ _____
  - ○ _____
- _____

Tell _____ to help people remember your points

A few types of speech openings:
- ✓ Ask a thought-provoking _____
- ✓ Make a startling _____
- ✓ Use a quote/_____
- ✓ Tell a _____
- ✓ Tell a relevant _____

A few types of Support Material:
- _____: Numerical ways of conveying information about incidents, data and events
- _____: Verifiable information (i.e. you didn't just make it up)
- _____: Quotes or opinions from experts
- _____: Relate events that happened to you or someone else
- _____: Diagrams, charts, pictures, models

7 Fundamental Motivators: SSCCRAL

S_____ going, going . . .

S_____ —peer pressure

C_____ -- I said I would

C_____ -- This is how I am/what I believe

R_____ -- others do unto you as you have done unto them

A_____ -- someone people respect/believe

L_____ -- I like you

The most persuasive word in the English language: _____

The LEAP process for conflict resolution:

L_____, E_____, A_____, P_____

Key point #1 in humor: People laugh when their minds are successfully

_____.

Practice, Practice, _____.

Lesson 16: Rhetorical Devices

SCREAM to Give Your Presentations Power!

Simile—using "like" or "as" to compare (sort of a gentler form of a metaphor)
He screamed like a little girl. He hid under the table, as quiet as a mouse.

Contrast—pairing of opposites
Churchill: There is only one answer to <u>defeat</u> and that is <u>victory</u>.   (It's a bonus if you can also use alliteration. For example: From the depths of <u>tragedy</u>, he rose to <u>triumph</u>)
Some opposite pairs: Present—Past (or Future), Beginning—End, Dark—Light, Friend—Foe.

Rhyme
Benjamin Franklin: An apple a <u>day</u> keeps the doctor <u>away</u>.

Echo: Repetition of a word or phrase

Churchill: <u>We shall fight</u> on the beaches, <u>we shall fight</u> on the landing grounds, <u>we shall fight</u> in the streets, <u>we shall fight</u> in the hiss; <u>we shall</u> never surrender.

Alliteration—repetition of the beginning sounds of a word.
Martin Luther King, Jr.: I have a dream that my little children will one day live in a nation where they will be judged not by the <u>c</u>olor of their skin but by the <u>c</u>ontent of their <u>c</u>haracter.

Metaphor—directly says that something is something else.
His beard was a lion's mane.
Bullets of hate shot from his mouth.
His bark is worse than his bite.
You can even combine rhetorical devices:

Shakespeare (Romeo speaking of Juliet):

"O, she doth teach the torches to burn bright! (Metaphor—Juliet is so radiant)
Her beauty hangs upon the cheek of night, (Metaphor—dark night sets off bright beauty)
Like a rich jewel in an Ethiop's ear"; (Simile—another expression of above metaphor).

Next Speech-- Use a minimum of 3 of the above rhetorical devices

Label them on your outline

Lesson 17: Interpretive Reading
Prose, Poetry, Oratorical speeches, Readers Theater, Monodrama

Do:
- Read someone else's material—this is not to be an original speech
- Include an introduction and conclusion to the excerpt
- Select material of interest to you and your audience
- Select material that will "show off" your vocal expression: tone, volume, rhythm, inflection
- Practice several times—At least twice alone and twice in front of someone else
- Use different voices for different characters (if more than one character). Don't do accents or different voices if you can't do it well. Select material accordingly.
- OK if you want to combine efforts with other students, as long as your contribution is approximately equal (adjust time accordingly)
- Consider re-typing material to be in a larger font with words underlined for emphasis and line breaks or other pauses indicated (. . . or /)

Don't:
- Memorize—this is a READING of the material (except for the introduction and conclusion).
- Worry about eye contact—the focus is on your voice.
- Think you can slack off on practicing. Practice is CRITICAL for this type of presentation.

Speech #9: Interpretive Reading selection

Interpretive Reading Activity: The Scorpion and the Frog

Readers Theater for 7 students
The Scorpion and the Frog
Author unknown, ancient tale

Reader 1:
One day, a scorpion looked around at the mountain where he lived and decided that he wanted a change.

Reader 2:
So he set out on a journey through the forests and hills. He climbed over rocks and under vines and kept going until he reached a river.

Reader 3: The river was wide and swift, and the scorpion stopped to reconsider the situation. He couldn't see any way across.

Reader 6: So he ran upriver and then checked downriver, all the while thinking that he might have to turn back.

Reader 7: Suddenly, he saw a frog sitting in the rushes by the bank of the stream on the other side of the river. He decided to ask the frog for help getting across the stream.

Reader 4 (Scorpion):

"Hellooo, Mr. Frog!" called the scorpion across the water, "Would you be so kind as to give me a ride on your back across the river?"

Reader 5 (Frog):

"Well now, Mr. Scorpion! How do I know that if I try to help you, you won't try to *kill* me?" asked the frog hesitantly.

Reader 4 (Scorpion):

"Because," the scorpion replied, "If I try to kill you, then I would die too, for you see I cannot swim!"

Reader 5 (Frog):

Now this seemed to make sense to the frog. But he asked. "What about when I get close to the bank? You could still try to kill me and get back to the shore!"

Reader 4 (Scorpion):

"This is true," agreed the scorpion, "But then I wouldn't be able to get to the other side of the river!"

Reader 5 (Frog):

"Alright then...how do I know you won't just wait till we get to the other side and THEN kill me?" said the frog.

Reader 4 (Scorpion):

"Ahh...," crooned the scorpion, "Because you see, once you've taken me to the other side of this river, I will be so grateful for your help, that it would hardly be fair to reward you with death, now would it?!"

Reader 1

So the frog agreed to take the scorpion across the river. He swam over to the bank and settled himself near the mud to pick up his passenger.

Reader 2 The scorpion crawled onto the frog's back, his sharp claws prickling into the frog's soft hide, and the frog slid into the river.

Reader 3 The muddy water swirled around them, but the frog stayed near the surface so the scorpion would not drown.

Reader 6 He kicked strongly through the first half of the stream, his flippers paddling wildly against the current.

Reader 7

Halfway across the river, the frog suddenly felt a sharp sting in his back and, out of the corner of his eye, saw the scorpion remove his stinger from the frog's back. A deadening numbness began to creep into his limbs.

Reader 5 (Frog):

"You fool!" croaked the frog, "Now we shall both die! Why on earth did you do that?"

Reader 4 (Scorpion):

The scorpion shrugged, and did a little jig on the drowning frog's back.

"I could not help myself. It is my nature."

Reader 1:

Then they both sank into the muddy waters of the swiftly flowing river.

Lesson 18: Using Dialogue

Narration tells. Dialogue shows.

It's the difference between saying "I told Tyler to look out for the truck," or me saying, "Tyler, look out for the truck!"

Example

Narration: When a girl wore the cat mask she was thinking about wearing for her speech, her friend took a picture with her phone, saying it would be a "purr-fect" Facebook post.

Basics of written dialogue:

1. Place quotation marks around the words that actually come out of the character's mouth.

The girl, wearing a cat mask, said, "I thought I'd wear this mask for my speech about cats."

2. Each time a person speaks, begin a new paragraph.

The girl, wearing a cat mask, said, "I thought I'd wear this mask for my speech about cats."

Her friend pulled out her phone and said, "This is purr-fect to post on Facebook!"

Basics of spoken dialogue:

Spoken dialogue is ACTING out the parts, using character voices, pauses, reactions, etc.

1.   Try to reduce the "he said/she said" parts and just say the actual words!

2.   Change character voices/position each time a different person speaks—Show the visual reaction before the verbal reaction

[Girl one, wearing a cat mask] "I thought I'd wear this mask for my speech about cats."
[Remove mask, turn slightly and take out cell phone, Girl two] "This is purr-fect to post on Facebook!"
Speech #10: Include a personal story with a dialogue of at least 4 lines between 2 characters (at least 2 characters talk back and forth with at least 4 lines of dialogue between them)

Note: for the 2 sessions **after** this one, the evaluators will interview the speakers near the start of the meeting and introduce the speaker (use this form) as well as provide an evaluation, if time allows.

Lesson 19: Introducing a Speaker

A good introduction fuses Subject, Audience and Speaker
- **S**ubject:
- **A**udience information (timely?/important?):
- **S**peaker's Credentials (education/experience/recognition):
- Title of Speech:
- Title of Speaker:
- Speaker's Name:
- Pronunciation:

Sample intro template: *{Approach lectern, face audience}*

1. Attention-getting opening: story/quote/startling fact/problem statement:

2. **Today, I am pleased to Introduce** _____[speaker's name—pronunciation)

3. **who is** [speaker's title or credentials—why they are the "expert"-- experience/education/awards or why they are speaking on this topic)

4. **Today we are going to find out** (hook the audience with a tease/preview/benefits)

5. "_____"[Title of Presentation], _____[Speaker's Name]

{Lead applause, wait for the speaker, shake hands, cross behind and sit down}

Turn in this sheet (filled-in) as your outline for this speech project. Also turn in the memorized portion.

Lesson 20: The Memorized Historical Speech

Introduction—does not have to be memorized
- Attention-getting opening (quote, startling statement, story, thought-provoking question):

- Author of original speech:

- Context of speech
  - Purpose of original speech (historical context):

  - Audience:

  - Location:

  - Date:

Body: 2-3 minute excerpt (cut portion) of a historical speech—Memorized: Write out (or type) on a separate sheet to turn in.

Conclusion—does not have to be memorized
- Impact of Speech (on the original audience, to History and even to today)

- Summary

- Closing Thought (Quote, Call to Action, Thought-provoking Statement, Rhetorical Question):

Source ideas:
- American Rhetoric: Top 100 American Speeches of the 20th Century (with transcripts!) http://www.americanrhetoric.com/top100speechesall.html
- Other historical speeches: The Gettysburg address, Winston Churchill speeches, Patrick Henry's "Give me Liberty or Give Me Death"

How to Memorize a Speech Word for Word

First, write the outline

Second, write (type or longhand) the body, then the introduction followed by the conclusion. Does it flow? Especially work on transitions.

Third, read your written speech out loud. Does it sound OK? Record, if possible. You can use the recorder on your cell phone.

Fourth—Apply memorization techniques:

Technique #1: CHUNK IT! Read, Recall, Check, Repeat

- Chunk the speech into smaller pieces (2-3 sentences)
- Read the chunk aloud
- Recall-try to say the chunk without peeking at the written speech
- Check by reading again (or if you recorded, you can listen to the recording)
- Repeat until you get the first chunk down
- Then go on to the next chunk of material, but include the first chunk in the "Recall" part: Chunk 1 + Chunk 2, then Chunk 1 + Chunk 2 + Chunk 3 and so on.
- Continue until you can say the entire speech, word for word

Technique #2: Silly Walk Method

1. Break the speech up into the main points

2. Assign each of the points to a room in your home—the sub points can be pieces of furniture

3. Create a Word Picture for the point. In your mind see yourself doing something silly with the word picture in the room.

4. Physically walk through the house if you can, picturing the silly pictures as you say the words for each point

5. Practice each segment, in order, several times, until you have the wording down (you can apply the Read, Recall, Check Repeat method here also)

Another version of the "Silly Walk" is to create a Map of your Speech and use pictures to represent concepts (or destinations) for your points.

Review Techniques: Speed Speech (saying the speech very fast), spaced reviews

MOST SPEECHES SHOULD <u>NOT</u> BE MEMORIZED WORD-FOR-WORD!

Lesson 21: Memorable Speeches Start with Strategic Structure

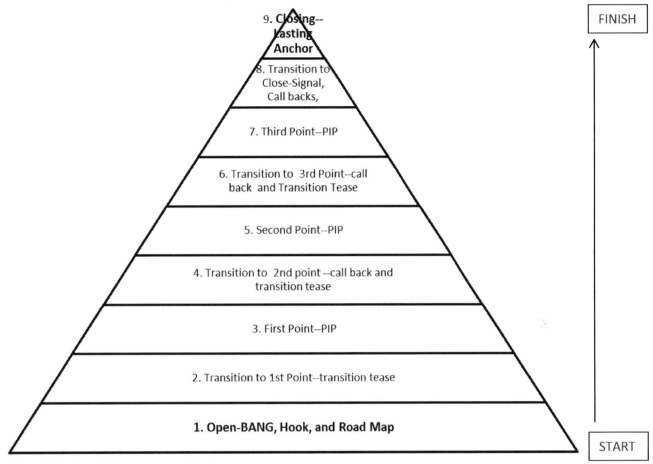

FINISH

9. Closing--Lasting Anchor

8. Transition to Close-Signal, Call backs,

7. Third Point--PIP

6. Transition to 3rd Point--call back and Transition Tease

5. Second Point--PIP

4. Transition to 2nd point --call back and transition tease

3. First Point--PIP

2. Transition to 1st Point--transition tease

1. Open-BANG, Hook, and Road Map

START

1 Open your speech with a BANG (question, startling statement, story) and then HOOK—the most important sentence of your speech—it gives the audience the reason why they should listen). Then, briefly give your audience a Road Map (preview) of where you will be taking them. You can list your points or provide an acronym. "Today you will learn the 4 tools of conflict resolution, designated by the acronym LEAP: Listen, Empathize, Agree and Partner."

2, 4, 6, 8 Transition to the next point by "calling back" the previous point(s) and then creating a desire for the next point by stating benefits of the point or asking questions to create a desire (Pain) that the point will resolve.   Prior to the closing, you will also want to signal the close: "Okay, to wrap it up" or "As we come to the end of the journey . . ." then call back (summarize) all points

3,5,7 Make your Points using PIP: Point, Illustrate, Practice
Point: Make Your Point, using a brief, memorable phrase (a foundational phrase) if possible (e.g. "Listen from Your Heart")
Illustrate: Use a mental anchor—Story, Analogy, Acronym, Demonstration
Practice: How and why will the people put the point into practice? Is this a point they need to practice? Do they need to reflect? Remember to answer the question WIIFM (What's In It For Me?)

9 Closing—Close with a Story (Circular—can "finish" a story), Quotation, Poem, Call for action, Question
→Use This Strategic Structure for Speech #12, Solving a Problem

Lesson 22: Dining Etiquette and Conversation

Discussion questions:

1. What information would you need to make a reservation at a restaurant? What is a maître d'? How do you indicate you are ready to order? How do you decide what to order if someone else is paying?

2.   Napkins: When do you put it on your lap? Where do you pit it if you need to temporarily leave the table? What are the primary uses of a napkin?

3. Silverware: Describe the uses of utensils (see diagram on next page). Where do you place the knife when eating? Where do you place the knife and fork to indicate that you are finished?

4. What conversation topics should be avoided? What are acceptable topics? Leaving a tip: What is an appropriate percentage? Why do we tip?

5. How do you eat the following items: soup, chicken on the bone, rolls with butter? (Describe what utensil to use and if there is a suggested method).

6.   Where would a woman place her purse? Where could she reapply lipstick or powder her nose? Is using a toothpick or comb acceptable at the table? What should you do if your cell phone rings?

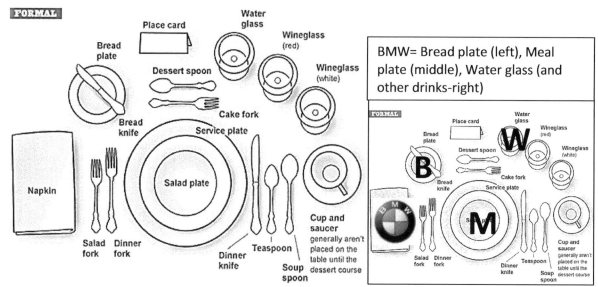

1. **Watch what others do**, especially the host. Don't start eating until the host starts. (Family Style: You can begin after everyone has received a little helping of each dish)

2. **Napkins go on the lap when you sit down** and on your seat when leaving the table temporarily. At the end of the meal, place the used napkin, semi-folded, to the left of your plate.

3. **Don't be a hick**: DON'T slurp liquids, burp, talk with your mouth full, pick at your teeth, lick fingers, rest elbows on the table, or wear a hat (unless outside).

4. **Passing:** Ask for items to be passed to you rather than stretching across people or the table (family style: pass to the right—counter-clockwise). Seconds can be passed in any direction. Pass salt and pepper together. Do not intercept a pass and snag an item for yourself.

REST

5. **Basic Utensil rules:** Work from the outside in. A fork may be used in the American style (switch hands) or Continental style (fork stays in the left hand). Once a utensil is used it should never touch the table, not even "planking" off the plate. **Used utensils rest on the plate**. When finished, they are placed parallel to each other at the "10 to 4" position. Eat soup by scooping the spoon away from you and sip from the side, not the end. Knives should never enter the mouth. Serving utensils: Always use serving utensils to serve yourself, not your personal utensils. Do not use butter and condiment serving utensils on your own food. Transfer a portion to your plate and then use your own utensil to spread.

DONE

6. **Bite-size it**. Most food should be cut into small, bite-sized pieces, if possible. Do not cut up an entire serving of meat. Cut 1-3 pieces at a time. Rolls should be torn into bite-sized pieces (only tear one piece at a time). Each piece is individually buttered.

7. **Taste food BEFORE adding salt and pepper**. To do otherwise insults the cook.

8. **Dinner partners rule!** Generally speaking, do not talk on the phone, text, listen to music or read at the table. If an urgent matter arises and you must attend to it, step away from the table.

9. **Dinner conversation tips:**
   a. Think before you speak
   b. Don't interrupt
   c. Don't monopolize the conversation. Encourage others to talk by asking open-ended questions.
   d. Don't say anything distasteful (gross, cursing, controversial).
   e. No negative comments about the food. Try at least a small portion of everything being served.

10. **Thank the host!**

Lesson 23: Brainstorming!

Brainstorm to generate (not judge!) ideas
Brainstorming "rules"

1. Cut criticism
2. Quantity over quality
3. Extend and Elaborate
4. Weird is wonderful

Individual brainstorming:

Free Association—write down whatever comes to mind
Mind Maps

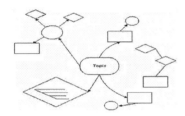

Group Brainstorming –a general topic for the Solve a Problem speech

(can be challenging if people feel shy or there are a few outspoken people)
Set ground rules and goals

Collaboration—bounce ideas off others

Encourage all ideas

Round Robin options
      O Verbal—each person states one idea in turn, and then can go around
      again
      O Anonymous—everyone write an idea on a slip of paper and turn in
      O Chain—pass paper around and everyone add 1-3 ideas (Brainwriting)

Solve a Problem/Offer a Solution Speech

Use the structure from Lesson 21
Consider how to be persuasive
Monroe's Motivated Sequence—for the persuasive speech!

7. **Attention**: Hey! Listen to me, you have a PROBLEM!
8. **Need**: Let me EXPLAIN the problem.
9. **Satisfy**: But, I have a SOLUTION!
10. **Visualization**: If we IMPLEMENT my solution, this is what will happen. Or, if we don't implement my solution, this is what will happen.
11. **Action**: You can help me in this specific way. Can you help me?
12. **Rebuttal**: Other people may say this, but MY solution is best.

Problem:

Research:

Solution:

Lesson 24 Group Problem Solving and Consensus

"In any moment of decision the best thing you can do is the right thing, the next best thing is the wrong thing, and the worst thing you can do is nothing." (Attributed to Theodore Roosevelt)

Whether you agree or disagree with the above quote, you still need to make decisions in life!

Basic Decision-Making Process

1. Define and clarify the issue.
   a. What are your choices?
   b. Is the matter urgent, important or both?
2. Research (get the facts and understand them)
3. Brainstorm
4. Consider Pros and Cons (2-sided list)
5. Select the best option (later, with new information and experience you may change)

Group Consensus Building

1. **Frame the decision as a "we" goal**

"What are the decisions we need to make?"

2. **Encourage participation**

"So, what do you think?"

3. **Use reflective listening**

4. **Summarize frequently**

"So, this is what we agree on. . ."

5. **If consensus appears near, test consensus**

"How are we doing?"

"Is there anything that is still a problem?"

The "Thumbs" method Thumbs Up = agreement; Thumbs Sideways = have concerns, but can support. Thumbs Down = don't agree and won't support.

Lesson 25: The Panel Discussion

Main Topic:_____

Panelist 1: name: _____ **sub topic:** _____

Panelist 2: name: _____ **sub topic:** _____

Panelist 3: name: _____ **sub topic:** _____

Panelist 4: name: _____ **sub topic:** _____

Panelist 5: name: _____ **sub topic:** _____

Panelist 6: name: _____ **sub topic:** _____

Panelist 7: name: _____ **sub topic:** _____

Panelist8: name: _____ **sub topic:** _____

Panelist 9: name: _____ **sub topic:** _____

Panelist 10: name: _____ **sub topic:** _____

Lesson 26: Selling a Product or Service

1. Understand Persuasion and Influence (Review Lesson 10)
2. Basic Tips:

- Know your product or service
- Practice, rehearse, role-play, script it out
- Plan your approach and revise with experience
- Be professional and friendly—appearance and likeability count!
    - SMILE, make eye-contact
- Use questions to identify needs—listen to the answers!
- Use FAB (Features/Advantages/Benefits)--Focus on BENEFITS
- Answer objections positively (I'm glad you mentioned that . . .)
- Ask for the sale! (Choice close—do you want the 8 pound one or the 10 pound one? Do you want me to mow once a week or twice?)
- Follow up and deliver what you promised
- Get testimonials from happy customers!
- Don't take rejection personally—it's a numbers game

The Principle of FAB: Features, Advantages, Benefits
People don't buy features (what something can do). People don't buy advantages (why it is better). People buy benefits—what the product's features and advantages will do for **them**.

Example: Let's say that you are selling cell phone plans . . .
A cell phone plan might have the feature of unlimited texts. The advantage is that you can send and receive unlimited texts. The benefit is that the person saves money (if going over the limit has been a problem), worry and possibly upset family relationships. It's the savings of money, worry and family relationships that the person buys. A sales person who focuses on those benefits will sell far more than a salesperson who simply sells "cell phone packages with unlimited texting."

The best way to sell to most people is to look at their NEED, from THEIR Viewpoint.
Remember WIIFM! (What's In It For Me?)
Activity:
Brainstorm ideas for products or services

- What?
- Target Market?
- Approach?
- Talking points for sales--FAB
- Role play

Lesson 27: Job Interviewing Tips—You are selling YOU!

1. Do some research on the company/person (internet, visit, talk to employees)
2. Review the job requirements carefully and focus planned responses on key words
3. Practice interview questions
4. Fill out applications neatly and completely. Check with references if it's OK to include them.
5. Dress neatly and be well-groomed.
6. Arrive early!
7. Greet the interviewer with eye contact, a smile and a handshake (practice). Be Polite!
8. Be prepared to elaborate on questions—don't just answer with a "Yes" or "No."
9. Always have at least one question to ask—even if it is just "What do you like about working here?"
10. Thank the interviewer and follow up with a thank you letter/email if you really want to impress!

Key interview questions:
Tell me about yourself . . .
    Keep your answer related to the job and only talk about your best traits. Practice a personal "commercial" for this question

Why are you interested in this job?
    Show that you have done your homework. State the positive things about the job and how they could further your personal or career goals.

Why should we hire you?
    This is a lot like "Tell me about yourself" but more focused on the benefits that you could bring to the position. Don't say, "I don't know."

What is your major weakness?
    Always turn this into a positive. Pick a weakness that could actually be a positive. "I have a tendency to be a perfectionist. I always want to see the job done right." Or pick a weakness that has nothing at all to do with the job. "My greatest weakness is milk chocolate."

What is your greatest strength?
    Here is a chance to highlight your best skills—focus on 3 or 4! Leadership, organization, communication (pick the skills that fit best for the position). Give examples.

How would you describe your ability as a team member?
    Give a positive example—sports, home, class, outside examples

Tell me about a major problem or difficult person you've handled recently
    Again, use a positive example that highlights a strength.

Interview Scenarios

BAD INTERVIEW Scenario for 2 people (give applicant cell phone)

Interviewer: (hold hand out to shake) *Hi, I'm _____*

Applicant: (slaps hand). *Hey, High Five!*

Interviewer: *You do realize you are about 15 minutes late, don't you?*

Applicant: (sitting down in a non-professional manner) *Yeah, I know. Traffic was terrible—I almost ran out of gas . . .I had to stop at a gas station. Finally, I got here and there was no parking, so I went ahead and parked in a handicapped spot.*

Interviewer: (sits down) *OK . . .well, I guess we can make this quick!*

Applicant: *Good . . . I was hoping this wouldn't take too long. . .hate to miss Dr. Phil, you know.*

Interviewer: *Dr. Phil?*

Applicant: *The talk show. Dr. Phil.*

Interviewer: *OK . . . Well, tell me what brought you here today. Why are you interested in working for InterTek?*

Applicant: *Well, I heard you were hiring and I really need a job.*

Interviewer: *Are you familiar with InterTek? Or the position?*

Applicant: *Well, not really. . Aren't you guys some computer geeks?*

Interviewer: *Well, not exactly. We process data. What are your computer skills?*

Applicant: (answering cell phone and talking to person on cell phone)
    What was your question?

Interviewer: *What are your computer skills? Why are you the best person for this data entry job?*

Applicant: *Skills . . . I have a lot of computer skills. I check my email every day. I do Facebook and YouTube. Yeah . . . I do a lot on the computer. How much does this job pay anyways?*

Interviewer: *The job pays $8-10/ hour, depending on your experience.*

Applicant: *Like I said I have a lot of computer skills, so let's just start me out at $10/hr.*

Interviewer: *Well, I have a few more questions . . .*

Applicant: *What about vacation? I need to know when I can start my vacation before I commit to this.*

Interviewer: *You know, we're going to have to cut this short today as you did come late. Plus I know you don't want to Dr. Phil!* (extend hand to shake)

Applicant: (slaps hand again) *I was getting tired of all those questions anyway. See ya!*

GOOD INTERVIEW Scenario (for 2 people)

Interviewer: (hold hand out to shake) *Hi, I'm _____.*

Applicant: (shakes hand) *Hi, I'm _____ here about the Data Entry job.*

Interviewer: *I saw you waiting in lobby and reading our company literature. I'm impressed you came early. Have a seat.*

Applicant: *Thanks. To tell you the truth, I was concerned that traffic might be bad, so I left extra early. I'm really interested in working for InterTek. You guys have a great reputation as one of the top, fast-growing data processing firms.*

Interviewer: *Yes, we do—sounds like you did your homework. Can you tell me a little about yourself?*

Applicant: *Sure! I'm a recent high school graduate. The classes I did the best in were business and computer-related. During high school I also had a part time job doing data entry for a computer-parts store. I prided myself on never being late for work. In my spare time, I enjoy reading and listening to music—at the same time, if possible!*

Interviewer: *In this economy, we have a lot of people applying for the data entry jobs. Some of them even have college degrees. Why do you think you're the best person for the job? Why should we hire you?*

Applicant: *I don't know about the other applicants, but there are 2 main reasons why I think I am a good fit for the job: 1. I have very good computer skills. I know all the main business applications, but most importantly for a data entry position, I have both speed and accuracy in keyboarding. I can type 100 words per minute, usually with no mistakes. And, 2. I'm dependable. As I mentioned, I've never been late for work. If you believe that time is money, then you will get a lot for your money with me!*

Interviewer: *You seem pretty confident for a recent high school graduate. What kind of pay do you need?*

Applicant: *That's a tough question. Can you tell me the range for this position?*

Interviewer: *The job pays $8-10/ hour, depending on your experience. Of course, there are promotion opportunities at InterTek—especially for go-getters like yourself!*

Applicant: *That's what I've heard and that's one of the reasons I'd really like to work for InterTek. I want to grow with the company. The $8-10 range is an acceptable range to start.*

Interviewer: *Do you have any other questions for me?*

Applicant: *Well, I'd love to know what you enjoy most about working here. . .*

Interviewer: *I guess it would be the people. We only hire skilled and motivated people. And we reward them well—which makes them even more motivated! And more fun to work with.* (Looking at watch). *Oh, our interview time is up. It has been a pleasure to meet you today* (extend hand—shake hands). *We will be contacting you by Friday if we have an offer.*

Applicant: *Thank you! I hope to be one of the people you enjoy working with!*

Lesson 28: Introduction to Debate

How to Win Arguments Using Debate Techniques
2 categories of arguments: offensive and defensive

1. **Offensive:** Advance an argument by making an ASSERTION, REASONS why and EVIDENCE. Establish why you should win. Why is change necessary? What are the reasons your solution will work? What evidence supports your reasoning?

A: Assertion   **"The death penalty is justified."**
R: Reasoning   **". . . because it reduces crime.**
E: Evidence   **"University studies conducted across the nation strongly point to this effect."**

You need all 3 parts of A.R.E for an effective argument. What's missing in #2 and #3?

	Assertion	Reasoning (the because)	Evidence
1	The minimum driving age should be raised to 18.	Raising the driving age will save lives by reducing accidents.	16-year-old drivers have 3 times as many crashes as drivers aged 18 and 19.
2	Video games are a bad influence.	Video games are too violent.	
3	Animals should not be dissected in school classes.		

2. **Defensive:** Why you should not lose. Change is not necessary. The other side's arguments do not apply. The other side has faulty reasoning. The other side is misinterpreting the evidence. To refute arguments, use a 4-step method:

Step 1: "They say . . ." Reference the argument. A debate can contain many arguments. By restating (paraphrasing or summarizing) the argument you are about to refute, you make it easier for people to follow your line of thinking.

Step 2: "But I disagree . . ." State the basics of your counter-argument. I can be the opposite stance or an attack on the reasoning or evidence.

Step 3: "Because . . ." Offer reasoning and evidence, if possible.

Step 4: "Therefore . . ." Draw a conclusion that compares your refutation to your opponent's argument and show why yours effectively defeats theirs. You need to show that your argument is better because
It is more logical ● It has better evidence ● It is more significant (it matters more or applies to more people)●It is consistent with experience: "Hey, we can all relate to this, right?"

Speaker 1: Bananas are better than oranges because they contain more potassium.

Speaker 2: Speaker 1 says that bananas are better than oranges, but I disagree.
Oranges are better than bananas because they contain more vitamin C. Therefore, you should prefer oranges because while many foods in an ordinary diet contain potassium, few contain an appreciable amount of vitamin C. It is more important to eat oranges whenever possible than it is to eat bananas.

Tracking Arguments—Simplified Debate

Proposition Speaker (speech)	Cross Ex. (1 min) & Opposition refutation (1-2 min)	Proposition rebuttal, 1-2 min

Tracking Arguments—Simplified Debate

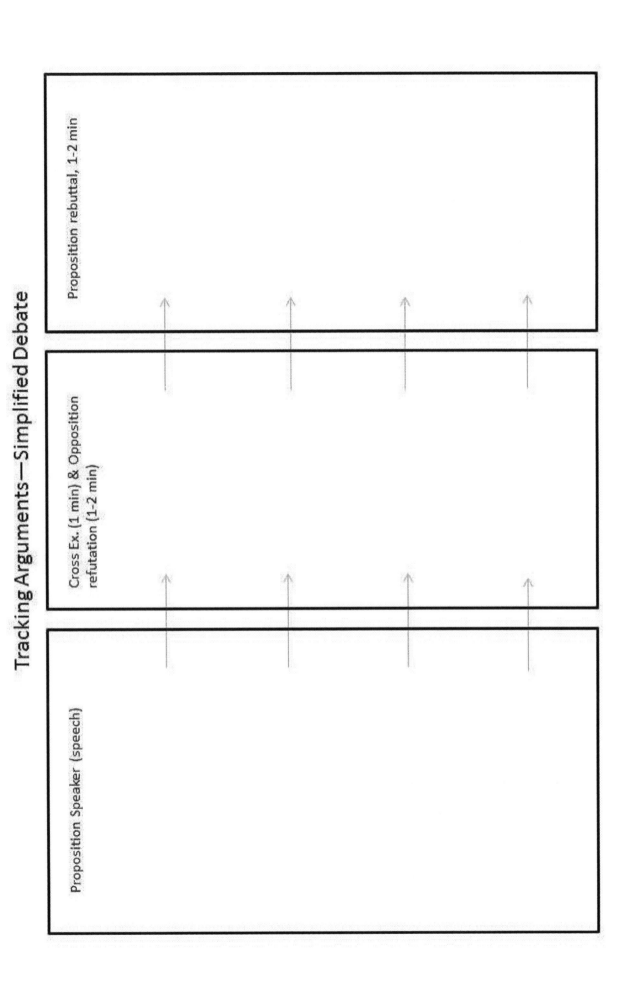

Proposition Speaker (speech)

Cross Ex. (1 min) & Opposition refutation (1-2 min)

Proposition rebuttal, 1-2 min

Tracking Arguments—Simplified Debate

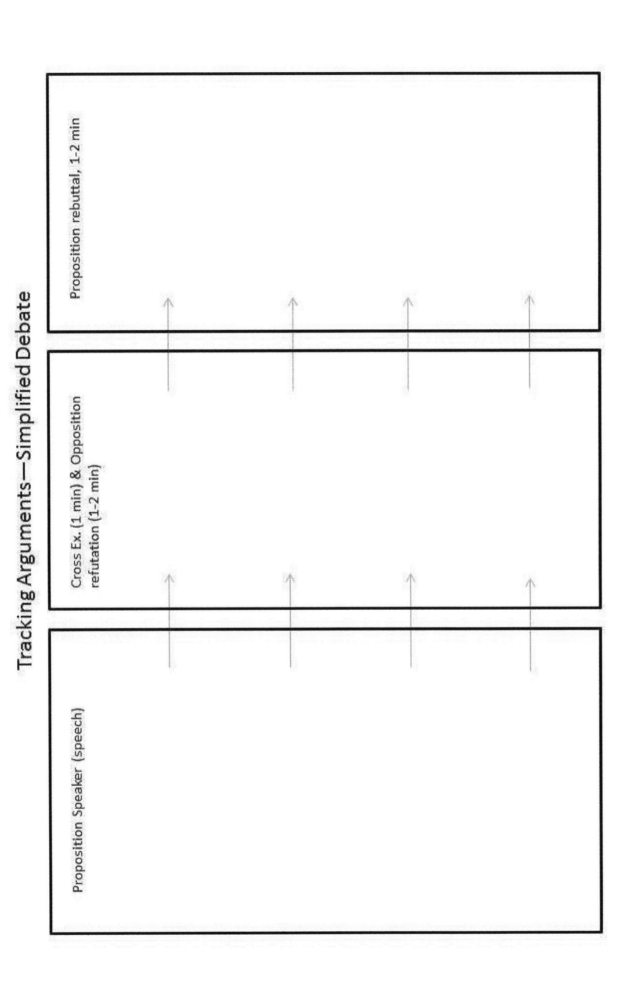

| Proposition Speaker (speech) | Cross Ex. (1 min) & Opposition refutation (1-2 min) | Proposition rebuttal, 1-2 min |

Appendix 1: Lesson Notes

Lesson 1: Introduction.
Students will not be giving prepared speeches, so the activities and going over the class format and expectations will take most of the time. If time allows, lead a session of impromptu speaking.

Fill-in-the-blanks:
Every speech has 3 main aspects: <u>Purpose</u>, <u>Content</u>, <u>Delivery</u>.
Your specific purpose—<u>your message</u>.
Determine what you want your audience to <u>think</u>, <u>feel</u> or <u>do</u>.
Write out your speech <u>word</u> for <u>word</u>.
Talk to <u>people</u> not <u>paper</u>.
The best speaking advice I've ever received: <u>Make a point. Tell a Story.</u>

Lesson 2: Evaluate to Motivate (1/2 students give Speech 1: Icebreaker)
Agenda change: This lesson should be done prior to student speeches, so that the evaluators can put the information into practice right away! Stress that evaluations should be supportive, friendly, honest and specific, ending on a positive note.

Lesson 3: Organizing a Speech (1/2 students give Speech 1: Icebreaker)
Point out the similarities between organizing a speech and writing a paper. Let students know that they may use prior papers as speech material.

Lesson 4: Ways to Start (and End) a Speech (1/2 Students give Speech 2: Organized Speech)

Fill-in-the-blanks:
5 Types of speech openings/closings:
Ask a thought-provoking <u>question.</u>
Make a startling <u>statement.</u>
Use a quote/<u>poem.</u>
Tell a <u>story.</u>
Tell a relevant <u>joke.</u>

A couple other closings: <u>circular</u> and <u>call for action</u>

Lesson 5: Effective Eye Contact—the Keyword Method (1/2 Students give Speech 2: Organize Your Speech)
Have the students read the paragraph "The Effects of Music on Plants" silently to themselves, marking the end of each sentence with a slash. Then, they can pick 3-4 key words per sentence to write on the next page. OK TO MAKE SYMBOLS (symbols are "free" and don't count in the key word count) After about 5 minutes, the students should "give a speech" to a partner using the keywords.

For the remaining speeches of the semester, limit the number of words on note cards—First limit to 100 words and then limit further in the second semester (30 words, for example)

Lesson 6: Vocal Variety (1/2 Students give Speech #3 Eye Contact)
A calculator may be needed.

Fill-in-the-blanks:
Pleasant, belly button, monotone.
For the "Your Turn" problem:
1:40 is 100 seconds.   [(200 words)/(100 seconds)] X 60 seconds/min = 120 WPM
120 WPM X 5 minutes = 600 words

Lesson 7: Your Body Speaks: Body Language and Props (1/2 students give Speech #3 Eye Contact)

Fill-in-the-blanks:
Nose, Open body language, Smile, Eye Contact
Practice, Practice, Practice!

Lesson 8: Using Storytelling to Craft Compelling Presentations (1/2 students give Speech #4 Vocal Variety)

Fill-in-the-blanks:
People remember stories. Stories tap into emotions. Stories are concrete. Stories connect you to your listener. As a presenter, or in conversation, stories are easy to remember.

For the Your Turn! worksheet, Students are to recall a story of someone who made a difference to them and then share it with a partner.

Lesson 9: Research your Topic (1/2 students give Speech #4 Vocal Variety)

Fill-in-the-blanks: Start with what you already know.

Activity: give students copies of related short articles, have them individually read the articles and then in groups of 3-4 combine the ideas into a single outline.

Lesson 10: Influence and Persuasion (1/2 students give Speech # 5 Body Language)

Fill-in-the-blanks:
7 Fundamental Motivators
Scarcity going, going . . .
Social proof—peer pressure
Commitment
Consistency
Reciprocity
Authority
Likeability

Activity: Students role play parent/child with child trying to persuade parent to do something (like extend curfew) using at least 2 of the 7 motivators.

Lesson 11: Conflict Resolution (1/2 students give Speech #5 Body Language)

Start the lessons with Scenarios 1 and 2, and then go through the worksheet, through the Fight-Flight-Freeze-Face section. Students should apply the information to their own situations (can have discussion). Then do scenario 3 and end with the worksheet section on LEAP for their own situations.

Lesson 12: Basic Humor Tips for Public Speaking (1/2 students give Speech # 6 Research Your Topic)
Fill-in-the-blanks:
People laugh when their minds are successfully <u>tricked</u>.
<u>Timing </u>is everything
You need to pause <u>before </u>the punch line!
You need to pause <u>after</u> the punch line.
Rule of 3. Have 3 items in a series, the first 2 being <u>logical</u> (the "set up") and the 3rd causing a <u>change</u> in direction.
I was nervous about the trip so I took a flashlight, a blanket, and . . . <u>my mother</u>.

The students can then brainstorm 10 logical essentials And 10 exaggerated essentials to come up with a "rule of 3" humorous statement "To be a persuasive speaker you need . . .)

Also talk about deprecating humor as being "safe" humor that endears you to your audience (see other worksheet)

 Lesson 13: Tell Your Testimony (1/2 students give Speech #6 Research Your Topic)
Although a Christian Testimony is given as an example, a product or service testimony can also fulfill the speech project.

Lesson 14: Skits and Readers Theater (1/2 students give speech #7 Tell Your Testimony)
A Christian skit is used. A non-religious skit could be substituted.

Lesson 15: Improv Games (1/2 students give speech #7 Tell Your Testimony)
This typically would be the last session of the first semester. For more improv game ideas, see: http://improvencyclopedia.org

Review sheet: no answers are given, but they can be easily found in the material. This optional review sheet can also be extra credit.

Lesson 16: Rhetorical Devices (no speeches)
This typically would be the first session of the second semester and as such, there would be no student speeches scheduled. In lieu of student speeches, a longer activity that encourages creativity and team work is encouraged. See the Marshmallow Challenge in Appendix 2.

Lesson 17: Interpretive Reading (1/2 students give speech #8 Rhetorical Devices)
Stress that the selection must be practiced and students do need to provide some sort of introduction and conclusion to the selection.   The "Scorpion and the Frog" Readers Theater is provided for practice in class.

Lesson 18: Using Dialogue (1/2 Students give Speech #8 Rhetorical Devices)
Optional warm-up activity: grab some simple comics and blank out the words in the word bubbles and have students come up with their own dialogue.

Lesson 19: Introducing a speaker (1/2 Students give Speech # 9 Interpretive Reading)
For the two classes after this lesson, the evaluators will also introduce the speaker they are evaluating. The impromptu segment may need to be reduced or eliminated to adjust for timing in lessons 20 & 21.

Lesson 20: The Memorized Historical Speech (1/2 Students give speech #9 Interpretive Reading)
Remember to allow time for the evaluators to talk with the speakers for their introductions. The impromptu segment may need to be reduced or eliminated to adjust for timing. For this speech project, students will excerpt a historical speech and provide an introduction and conclusion to give historical context and lasting impact.

Lesson 21: Memorable Speeches Start with Strategic Structure (1/2 students give Speech #10 Story with Dialogue)
Remember to allow time for the evaluators to talk with the speakers for their introductions. The impromptu segment may need to be reduced or eliminated to adjust for timing.

This structure may be too detailed for very short speeches. This structure should be used for speech #12, solving a problem

Lesson 22: Dining Etiquette and Conversation (1/2 students give Speech #10 Story with Dialogue)
Begin the lesson with dividing the discussion questions among the students. Each grouping of students can have 1 or 2 questions. Each group will report on their discussion to the whole class. This activity can be shrunk or stretched to fit the time. Suggestion: Bring a napkin, knife and fork to demonstrate.

Lesson 23: Brainstorming! (1/2 students give Speech #11 Memorized Historical Speech)
In addition to a lesson on brainstorming, the students will use some of the techniques to brainstorm a general topic and enough subtopics for each student to pick a topic for speech #12, the Problem/solution speeches. This process may be continued in the next lesson. These speeches will be recycled for the debates (yes, that means that the 14th speech is a re-do of the 12th speech).

Lesson 24: Group Problem Solving and Consensus (1/2 students give Speech #11 Memorized Historical Speech)
This lesson can be a continuation of Lesson 23, including a group consensus on a topic of the students' choice.

Lesson 25: The Panel Discussion (1/2 students give Speech #12 Structure/Problem)
Half of the students will present Speech #12 and the other half will take notes. No evaluations. Instead of evaluations, the "evaluators" will ask questions and summarize the speeches.

Lesson 26: Selling a Product or Service (1/2 students give Speech #12 Structure/Problem)
Half of the students will present Speech #12 and the other half will take notes. No evaluations. Instead of evaluations, the "evaluators" will ask questions and summarize the speeches.
Suggestion for lesson activity: have unusual or even ordinary objects and have the students use FAB to sell them to the group.

Lesson 27: Job Interviewing Tips: You are Selling You! (1/2 Students give Speech #13 Sell a Product or Service)

Suggest to next week's impromptu leader to pick interview questions as impromptu topics.

Lesson 28: Introduction to Debate (1/2 Students give Speech #13 Sell a Product or Service)

This is a very limited introduction to debate. Classes 29 and 30 will use a modified debate form in which the "evaluator" will cross examine (ask questions) of the speaker and then refute the speakers points. The speaker will then have a rebuttal opportunity.

Classes 29 and 30: Using the speeches originally prepared for Speech #12 Solve a problem (the speeches which were all related to the same topic), half of the students will present Speech #14 one week and the other half the following week, with the "evaluators" taking the opposing view instead of doing evaluations.

Appendix 2: The Marshmallow Challenge

Developed by Tom Wujec

For more information (including presentation materials): http://marshmallowchallenge.com

Preparation

In advance of the class, create a marshmallow challenge kit for each team (2-4 students), with each kit containing twenty sticks of spaghetti, one yard of masking tape, one yard of string and one marshmallow. These ingredients should be placed into a paper lunch bag, which simplifies distribution and hides the contents, maximizing the element of surprise.

✦ Spaghetti: Ensure that you use uncooked spaghetti. Avoid spaghettini as it is too thin and breaks easily. Fettuccini is too thick.

✦ String: Include string that can be easily broken by hand. If the string is thick, include scissors in your kit.

✦ Marshmallow: Use a name brand or private label brand of marshmallows that measure the 'standard' size, about an inch and a half across. Avoid mini or jumbo marshmallows. Also avoid stale marshmallows. You'll want squishy marshmallows that give the impression of lightness.

✦ Masking Tape: Get standard masking tape. Generally, you'll want to put the tape on the side of the table, the back of a chair or a nearby wall. Rolling it in the bag tangles the tape.

✦ Paper Lunch Bags: Standard size lunch bags work well as do letter size manila envelopes.

Also ensure that you have the following tools to run the challenge:

✦ Measuring Tape: Have a contractor's retractable measuring available after the challenge is finished so you can measure the height of the structures.

✦ Countdown Application or Stopwatch: The actual marshmallow challenge takes eighteen minutes. Eighteen minutes seems to be the magic time. Twenty minutes is too long and fifteen is too short.

Give Clear Instructions

Be clear about the goals and rules of the Marshmallow Challenge.

✦ Build the Tallest Freestanding Structure: The winning team is the one that has the tallest structure measured from the table top surface to the top of the marshmallow. That means the structure cannot be suspended from a higher structure, like a chair, ceiling or chandelier.

✦ The Entire Marshmallow Must be on Top: The entire marshmallow needs to be on the top of the structure. Cutting or eating part of the marshmallow disqualifies the team.

✦ Use as Much or as Little of the Kit: The team can use as many or as few of the 20 spaghetti sticks, as much or as little of the string or tape. The team cannot use the paper bag as part of their structure.

✦ Break up the Spaghetti, String or Tape: Teams are free to break the spaghetti, cut up the tape and string to create new structures.

✦ The Challenge Lasts 18 minutes: Teams cannot hold on to the structure when the time runs out. Those touching or supporting the structure at the end of the exercise will be disqualified.

✦ Ensure Everyone Understands the Rules: Don't worry about repeating the rules too many times.

Repeat them at least three times. Ask if anyone has any questions before starting.

Finish the Challenge—Declare a Winner!

After the clock runs out, ask everyone in the room to sit down so everyone can see the structures. Likely, just over half the teams will have standing structures.

✦ Measure the Structures: From the shortest standing structure to the tallest, measure and call out the heights. If you're documenting the challenge, have someone record the heights.

✦ Identify the Winning Team: Ensure they get a standing ovation and a prize (if you've offered one).

✦ Wrap up with the Lessons of the Marshmallow Challenge

✦ Kids do Better than Business Students: On virtually every measure of innovation, kindergarteners create taller and more interesting structures.

Appendix 3: Agendas

Available online:
http://bit.ly/Speechclassagenda

Date:	
Announcements	
Warm-up Activity	
Speakers Turn in Checklist & Outline	
Grammarian	
Word of the Day	
Timer	
Speaker 1	
Speaker 2	
Speaker 3	
Speaker 4	
Speaker 5	
Speaker 6	
Speaker 7	
Speaker 8	
Speaker 9	
Speaker 10	
Evaluator 1	
Evaluator 2	
Evaluator 3	
Evaluator 4	
Evaluator 5	
Evaluator 6	
Evaluator 7	
Evaluator 8	
Evaluator 9	
Evaluator 10	
Impromptu Leader	
Timer Report	
Grammarian Report	
Lesson	
Review Assignments	

Date:	
Announcements	
Warm-up Activity	
Speakers Turn in Checklist & Outline	
Grammarian	
Word of the Day	
Timer	
Speaker 1	
Speaker 2	
Speaker 3	
Speaker 4	
Speaker 5	
Speaker 6	
Speaker 7	
Speaker 8	
Speaker 9	
Speaker 10	
Evaluator 1	
Evaluator 2	
Evaluator 3	
Evaluator 4	
Evaluator 5	
Evaluator 6	
Evaluator 7	
Evaluator 8	
Evaluator 9	
Evaluator 10	
Impromptu Leader	
Timer Report	
Grammarian Report	
Lesson	
Review Assignments	

Date:	
Announcements	
Warm-up Activity	
Speakers Turn in Checklist & Outline	
Grammarian	
Word of the Day	
Timer	
Speaker 1	
Speaker 2	
Speaker 3	
Speaker 4	
Speaker 5	
Speaker 6	
Speaker 7	
Speaker 8	
Speaker 9	
Speaker 10	
Evaluator 1	
Evaluator 2	
Evaluator 3	
Evaluator 4	
Evaluator 5	
Evaluator 6	
Evaluator 7	
Evaluator 8	
Evaluator 9	
Evaluator 10	
Impromptu Leader	
Timer Report	
Grammarian Report	
Lesson	
Review Assignments	

Date:	
Announcements	
Warm-up Activity	
Speakers Turn in Checklist & Outline	
Grammarian	
Word of the Day	
Timer	
Speaker 1	
Speaker 2	
Speaker 3	
Speaker 4	
Speaker 5	
Speaker 6	
Speaker 7	
Speaker 8	
Speaker 9	
Speaker 10	
Evaluator 1	
Evaluator 2	
Evaluator 3	
Evaluator 4	
Evaluator 5	
Evaluator 6	
Evaluator 7	
Evaluator 8	
Evaluator 9	
Evaluator 10	
Impromptu Leader	
Timer Report	
Grammarian Report	
Lesson	
Review Assignments	

Date:	
Announcements	
Warm-up Activity	
Speakers Turn in Checklist & Outline	
Grammarian	
Word of the Day	
Timer	
Speaker 1	
Speaker 2	
Speaker 3	
Speaker 4	
Speaker 5	
Speaker 6	
Speaker 7	
Speaker 8	
Speaker 9	
Speaker 10	
Evaluator 1	
Evaluator 2	
Evaluator 3	
Evaluator 4	
Evaluator 5	
Evaluator 6	
Evaluator 7	
Evaluator 8	
Evaluator 9	
Evaluator 10	
Impromptu Leader	
Timer Report	
Grammarian Report	
Lesson	
Review Assignments	

Date:	
Announcements	
Warm-up Activity	
Speakers Turn in Checklist & Outline	
Grammarian	
Word of the Day	
Timer	
Speaker 1	
Speaker 2	
Speaker 3	
Speaker 4	
Speaker 5	
Speaker 6	
Speaker 7	
Speaker 8	
Speaker 9	
Speaker 10	
Evaluator 1	
Evaluator 2	
Evaluator 3	
Evaluator 4	
Evaluator 5	
Evaluator 6	
Evaluator 7	
Evaluator 8	
Evaluator 9	
Evaluator 10	
Impromptu Leader	
Timer Report	
Grammarian Report	
Lesson	
Review Assignments	

Date:	
Announcements	
Warm-up Activity	
Speakers Turn in Checklist & Outline	
Grammarian	
Word of the Day	
Timer	
Speaker 1	
Speaker 2	
Speaker 3	
Speaker 4	
Speaker 5	
Speaker 6	
Speaker 7	
Speaker 8	
Speaker 9	
Speaker 10	
Evaluator 1	
Evaluator 2	
Evaluator 3	
Evaluator 4	
Evaluator 5	
Evaluator 6	
Evaluator 7	
Evaluator 8	
Evaluator 9	
Evaluator 10	
Impromptu Leader	
Timer Report	
Grammarian Report	
Lesson	
Review Assignments	

Date:	
Announcements	
Warm-up Activity	
Speakers Turn in Checklist & Outline	
Grammarian	
Word of the Day	
Timer	
Speaker 1	
Speaker 2	
Speaker 3	
Speaker 4	
Speaker 5	
Speaker 6	
Speaker 7	
Speaker 8	
Speaker 9	
Speaker 10	
Evaluator 1	
Evaluator 2	
Evaluator 3	
Evaluator 4	
Evaluator 5	
Evaluator 6	
Evaluator 7	
Evaluator 8	
Evaluator 9	
Evaluator 10	
Impromptu Leader	
Timer Report	
Grammarian Report	
Lesson	
Review Assignments	

Date:	
Announcements	
Warm-up Activity	
Speakers Turn in Checklist & Outline	
Grammarian	
Word of the Day	
Timer	
Speaker 1	
Speaker 2	
Speaker 3	
Speaker 4	
Speaker 5	
Speaker 6	
Speaker 7	
Speaker 8	
Speaker 9	
Speaker 10	
Evaluator 1	
Evaluator 2	
Evaluator 3	
Evaluator 4	
Evaluator 5	
Evaluator 6	
Evaluator 7	
Evaluator 8	
Evaluator 9	
Evaluator 10	
Impromptu Leader	
Timer Report	
Grammarian Report	
Lesson	
Review Assignments	

Date:	
Announcements	
Warm-up Activity	
Speakers Turn in Checklist & Outline	
Grammarian	
Word of the Day	
Timer	
Speaker 1	
Speaker 2	
Speaker 3	
Speaker 4	
Speaker 5	
Speaker 6	
Speaker 7	
Speaker 8	
Speaker 9	
Speaker 10	
Evaluator 1	
Evaluator 2	
Evaluator 3	
Evaluator 4	
Evaluator 5	
Evaluator 6	
Evaluator 7	
Evaluator 8	
Evaluator 9	
Evaluator 10	
Impromptu Leader	
Timer Report	
Grammarian Report	
Lesson	
Review Assignments	

Date:	
Announcements	
Warm-up Activity	
Speakers Turn in Checklist & Outline	
Grammarian	
Word of the Day	
Timer	
Speaker 1	
Speaker 2	
Speaker 3	
Speaker 4	
Speaker 5	
Speaker 6	
Speaker 7	
Speaker 8	
Speaker 9	
Speaker 10	
Evaluator 1	
Evaluator 2	
Evaluator 3	
Evaluator 4	
Evaluator 5	
Evaluator 6	
Evaluator 7	
Evaluator 8	
Evaluator 9	
Evaluator 10	
Impromptu Leader	
Timer Report	
Grammarian Report	
Lesson	
Review Assignments	

Date:	
Announcements	
Warm-up Activity	
Speakers Turn in Checklist & Outline	
Grammarian	
Word of the Day	
Timer	
Speaker 1	
Speaker 2	
Speaker 3	
Speaker 4	
Speaker 5	
Speaker 6	
Speaker 7	
Speaker 8	
Speaker 9	
Speaker 10	
Evaluator 1	
Evaluator 2	
Evaluator 3	
Evaluator 4	
Evaluator 5	
Evaluator 6	
Evaluator 7	
Evaluator 8	
Evaluator 9	
Evaluator 10	
Impromptu Leader	
Timer Report	
Grammarian Report	
Lesson	
Review Assignments	

Date:	
Announcements	
Warm-up Activity	
Speakers Turn in Checklist & Outline	
Grammarian	
Word of the Day	
Timer	
Speaker 1	
Speaker 2	
Speaker 3	
Speaker 4	
Speaker 5	
Speaker 6	
Speaker 7	
Speaker 8	
Speaker 9	
Speaker 10	
Evaluator 1	
Evaluator 2	
Evaluator 3	
Evaluator 4	
Evaluator 5	
Evaluator 6	
Evaluator 7	
Evaluator 8	
Evaluator 9	
Evaluator 10	
Impromptu Leader	
Timer Report	
Grammarian Report	
Lesson	
Review Assignments	

Date:	
Announcements	
Warm-up Activity	
Speakers Turn in Checklist & Outline	
Grammarian	
Word of the Day	
Timer	
Speaker 1	
Speaker 2	
Speaker 3	
Speaker 4	
Speaker 5	
Speaker 6	
Speaker 7	
Speaker 8	
Speaker 9	
Speaker 10	
Evaluator 1	
Evaluator 2	
Evaluator 3	
Evaluator 4	
Evaluator 5	
Evaluator 6	
Evaluator 7	
Evaluator 8	
Evaluator 9	
Evaluator 10	
Impromptu Leader	
Timer Report	
Grammarian Report	
Lesson	
Review Assignments	

Date:	
Announcements	
Warm-up Activity	
Speakers Turn in Checklist & Outline	
Grammarian	
Word of the Day	
Timer	
Speaker 1	
Speaker 2	
Speaker 3	
Speaker 4	
Speaker 5	
Speaker 6	
Speaker 7	
Speaker 8	
Speaker 9	
Speaker 10	
Evaluator 1	
Evaluator 2	
Evaluator 3	
Evaluator 4	
Evaluator 5	
Evaluator 6	
Evaluator 7	
Evaluator 8	
Evaluator 9	
Evaluator 10	
Impromptu Leader	
Timer Report	
Grammarian Report	
Lesson	
Review Assignments	

Date:	
Announcements	
Warm-up Activity	
Speakers Turn in Checklist & Outline	
Grammarian	
Word of the Day	
Timer	
Speaker 1	
Speaker 2	
Speaker 3	
Speaker 4	
Speaker 5	
Speaker 6	
Speaker 7	
Speaker 8	
Speaker 9	
Speaker 10	
Evaluator 1	
Evaluator 2	
Evaluator 3	
Evaluator 4	
Evaluator 5	
Evaluator 6	
Evaluator 7	
Evaluator 8	
Evaluator 9	
Evaluator 10	
Impromptu Leader	
Timer Report	
Grammarian Report	
Lesson	
Review Assignments	

Date:	
Announcements	
Warm-up Activity	
Speakers Turn in Checklist & Outline	
Grammarian	
Word of the Day	
Timer	
Speaker 1	
Speaker 2	
Speaker 3	
Speaker 4	
Speaker 5	
Speaker 6	
Speaker 7	
Speaker 8	
Speaker 9	
Speaker 10	
Evaluator 1	
Evaluator 2	
Evaluator 3	
Evaluator 4	
Evaluator 5	
Evaluator 6	
Evaluator 7	
Evaluator 8	
Evaluator 9	
Evaluator 10	
Impromptu Leader	
Timer Report	
Grammarian Report	
Lesson	
Review Assignments	

Date:	
Announcements	
Warm-up Activity	
Speakers Turn in Checklist & Outline	
Grammarian	
Word of the Day	
Timer	
Speaker 1	
Speaker 2	
Speaker 3	
Speaker 4	
Speaker 5	
Speaker 6	
Speaker 7	
Speaker 8	
Speaker 9	
Speaker 10	
Evaluator 1	
Evaluator 2	
Evaluator 3	
Evaluator 4	
Evaluator 5	
Evaluator 6	
Evaluator 7	
Evaluator 8	
Evaluator 9	
Evaluator 10	
Impromptu Leader	
Timer Report	
Grammarian Report	
Lesson	
Review Assignments	

Date:	
Announcements	
Warm-up Activity	
Speakers Turn in Checklist & Outline	
Grammarian	
Word of the Day	
Timer	
Speaker 1	
Speaker 2	
Speaker 3	
Speaker 4	
Speaker 5	
Speaker 6	
Speaker 7	
Speaker 8	
Speaker 9	
Speaker 10	
Evaluator 1	
Evaluator 2	
Evaluator 3	
Evaluator 4	
Evaluator 5	
Evaluator 6	
Evaluator 7	
Evaluator 8	
Evaluator 9	
Evaluator 10	
Impromptu Leader	
Timer Report	
Grammarian Report	
Lesson	
Review Assignments	

Date:	
Announcements	
Warm-up Activity	
Speakers Turn in Checklist & Outline	
Grammarian	
Word of the Day	
Timer	
Speaker 1	
Speaker 2	
Speaker 3	
Speaker 4	
Speaker 5	
Speaker 6	
Speaker 7	
Speaker 8	
Speaker 9	
Speaker 10	
Evaluator 1	
Evaluator 2	
Evaluator 3	
Evaluator 4	
Evaluator 5	
Evaluator 6	
Evaluator 7	
Evaluator 8	
Evaluator 9	
Evaluator 10	
Impromptu Leader	
Timer Report	
Grammarian Report	
Lesson	
Review Assignments	

Date:	
Announcements	
Warm-up Activity	
Speakers Turn in Checklist & Outline	
Grammarian	
Word of the Day	
Timer	
Speaker 1	
Speaker 2	
Speaker 3	
Speaker 4	
Speaker 5	
Speaker 6	
Speaker 7	
Speaker 8	
Speaker 9	
Speaker 10	
Evaluator 1	
Evaluator 2	
Evaluator 3	
Evaluator 4	
Evaluator 5	
Evaluator 6	
Evaluator 7	
Evaluator 8	
Evaluator 9	
Evaluator 10	
Impromptu Leader	
Timer Report	
Grammarian Report	
Lesson	
Review Assignments	

Date:	
Announcements	
Warm-up Activity	
Speakers Turn in Checklist & Outline	
Grammarian	
Word of the Day	
Timer	
Speaker 1	
Speaker 2	
Speaker 3	
Speaker 4	
Speaker 5	
Speaker 6	
Speaker 7	
Speaker 8	
Speaker 9	
Speaker 10	
Evaluator 1	
Evaluator 2	
Evaluator 3	
Evaluator 4	
Evaluator 5	
Evaluator 6	
Evaluator 7	
Evaluator 8	
Evaluator 9	
Evaluator 10	
Impromptu Leader	
Timer Report	
Grammarian Report	
Lesson	
Review Assignments	

Date:	
Announcements	
Warm-up Activity	
Speakers Turn in Checklist & Outline	
Grammarian	
Word of the Day	
Timer	
Speaker 1	
Speaker 2	
Speaker 3	
Speaker 4	
Speaker 5	
Speaker 6	
Speaker 7	
Speaker 8	
Speaker 9	
Speaker 10	
Evaluator 1	
Evaluator 2	
Evaluator 3	
Evaluator 4	
Evaluator 5	
Evaluator 6	
Evaluator 7	
Evaluator 8	
Evaluator 9	
Evaluator 10	
Impromptu Leader	
Timer Report	
Grammarian Report	
Lesson	
Review Assignments	

Date:	
Announcements	
Warm-up Activity	
Speakers Turn in Checklist & Outline	
Grammarian	
Word of the Day	
Timer	
Speaker 1	
Speaker 2	
Speaker 3	
Speaker 4	
Speaker 5	
Speaker 6	
Speaker 7	
Speaker 8	
Speaker 9	
Speaker 10	
Evaluator 1	
Evaluator 2	
Evaluator 3	
Evaluator 4	
Evaluator 5	
Evaluator 6	
Evaluator 7	
Evaluator 8	
Evaluator 9	
Evaluator 10	
Impromptu Leader	
Timer Report	
Grammarian Report	
Lesson	
Review Assignments	

Date:	
Announcements	
Warm-up Activity	
Speakers Turn in Checklist & Outline	
Grammarian	
Word of the Day	
Timer	
Speaker 1	
Speaker 2	
Speaker 3	
Speaker 4	
Speaker 5	
Speaker 6	
Speaker 7	
Speaker 8	
Speaker 9	
Speaker 10	
Evaluator 1	
Evaluator 2	
Evaluator 3	
Evaluator 4	
Evaluator 5	
Evaluator 6	
Evaluator 7	
Evaluator 8	
Evaluator 9	
Evaluator 10	
Impromptu Leader	
Timer Report	
Grammarian Report	
Lesson	
Review Assignments	

Date:	
Announcements	
Warm-up Activity	
Speakers Turn in Checklist & Outline	
Grammarian	
Word of the Day	
Timer	
Speaker 1	
Speaker 2	
Speaker 3	
Speaker 4	
Speaker 5	
Speaker 6	
Speaker 7	
Speaker 8	
Speaker 9	
Speaker 10	
Evaluator 1	
Evaluator 2	
Evaluator 3	
Evaluator 4	
Evaluator 5	
Evaluator 6	
Evaluator 7	
Evaluator 8	
Evaluator 9	
Evaluator 10	
Impromptu Leader	
Timer Report	
Grammarian Report	
Lesson	
Review Assignments	

Date:	
Announcements	
Warm-up Activity	
Speakers Turn in Checklist & Outline	
Grammarian	
Word of the Day	
Timer	
Speaker 1	
Speaker 2	
Speaker 3	
Speaker 4	
Speaker 5	
Speaker 6	
Speaker 7	
Speaker 8	
Speaker 9	
Speaker 10	
Evaluator 1	
Evaluator 2	
Evaluator 3	
Evaluator 4	
Evaluator 5	
Evaluator 6	
Evaluator 7	
Evaluator 8	
Evaluator 9	
Evaluator 10	
Impromptu Leader	
Timer Report	
Grammarian Report	
Lesson	
Review Assignments	

Date:	
Announcements	
Warm-up Activity	
Speakers Turn in Checklist & Outline	
Grammarian	
Word of the Day	
Timer	
Speaker 1	
Speaker 2	
Speaker 3	
Speaker 4	
Speaker 5	
Speaker 6	
Speaker 7	
Speaker 8	
Speaker 9	
Speaker 10	
Evaluator 1	
Evaluator 2	
Evaluator 3	
Evaluator 4	
Evaluator 5	
Evaluator 6	
Evaluator 7	
Evaluator 8	
Evaluator 9	
Evaluator 10	
Impromptu Leader	
Timer Report	
Grammarian Report	
Lesson	
Review Assignments	

Date:	
Announcements	
Warm-up Activity	
Speakers Turn in Checklist & Outline	
Grammarian	
Word of the Day	
Timer	
Speaker 1	
Speaker 2	
Speaker 3	
Speaker 4	
Speaker 5	
Speaker 6	
Speaker 7	
Speaker 8	
Speaker 9	
Speaker 10	
Evaluator 1	
Evaluator 2	
Evaluator 3	
Evaluator 4	
Evaluator 5	
Evaluator 6	
Evaluator 7	
Evaluator 8	
Evaluator 9	
Evaluator 10	
Impromptu Leader	
Timer Report	
Grammarian Report	
Lesson	
Review Assignments	

Date:	
Announcements	
Warm-up Activity	
Speakers Turn in Checklist & Outline	
Grammarian	
Word of the Day	
Timer	
Speaker 1	
Speaker 2	
Speaker 3	
Speaker 4	
Speaker 5	
Speaker 6	
Speaker 7	
Speaker 8	
Speaker 9	
Speaker 10	
Evaluator 1	
Evaluator 2	
Evaluator 3	
Evaluator 4	
Evaluator 5	
Evaluator 6	
Evaluator 7	
Evaluator 8	
Evaluator 9	
Evaluator 10	
Impromptu Leader	
Timer Report	
Grammarian Report	
Lesson	
Review Assignments	

Date:	
Announcements	
Warm-up Activity	
Speakers Turn in Checklist & Outline	
Grammarian	
Word of the Day	
Timer	
Speaker 1	
Speaker 2	
Speaker 3	
Speaker 4	
Speaker 5	
Speaker 6	
Speaker 7	
Speaker 8	
Speaker 9	
Speaker 10	
Evaluator 1	
Evaluator 2	
Evaluator 3	
Evaluator 4	
Evaluator 5	
Evaluator 6	
Evaluator 7	
Evaluator 8	
Evaluator 9	
Evaluator 10	
Impromptu Leader	
Timer Report	
Grammarian Report	
Lesson	
Review Assignments	

Appendix 4: Assignment Sheets

Speaker Assignment

Name: _____   Date:_____

Speech # _____ Speech Assignment (icebreaker, etc.) _____

Title of Speech: _____

Speaker Assignment Sheet

Speakers: Students will present speeches as assigned. Typically, the subject is of the student's choosing, and may reflect a student's beliefs and values. However, all subjects and language used are to be respectful.

Preparation Checklist:

____ Review notes for assignment (icebreaker, organize your speech, Eye Contact, Vocal Variety, Body Language, Research Your Topic, Tell Your Testimony)

___Brainstorming

___Topic/Subject:

___Research, if necessary

___More Brainstorming, if necessary

___Trial Outline

- Main idea:
- Point 1:
    - O Support for Point 1:
    - O Support for Point 1:
- Point 2:
    - O Support for Point 2:
    - O Support for Point 2:
- Point 3 (optional):
    - O Support for Point 3:
    - O Support for Point 3:

___Write Introduction/Attention-getter

___Write Conclusion/Summary

___Write outline (to hand in)

___Write out Speech

___Read out loud

___Edit

___Reduce to Keywords (on cards)

___Practice in front of someone (get feedback)

   Signature of person: _____

___Revise

___Practice 2X or more

Turn in this sheet and your outline at the beginning of class!

Name: _____   Date:_____

Speech # _____ Speech Assignment (icebreaker, etc.) _____

Title of Speech: _____

Speaker Assignment Sheet

Speakers: Students will present speeches as assigned. Typically, the subject is of the student's choosing, and may reflect a student's beliefs and values. However, all subjects and language used are to be respectful.

Preparation Checklist:

____ Review notes for assignment (icebreaker, organize your speech, Eye Contact, Vocal Variety, Body Language, Research Your Topic, Tell Your Testimony)

___Brainstorming

___Topic/Subject:

___Research, if necessary

___More Brainstorming, if necessary

___Trial Outline
- Main idea:
- Point 1:
    - O Support for Point 1:
    - O Support for Point 1:
- Point 2:
    - O Support for Point 2:
    - O Support for Point 2:
- Point 3 (optional):
    - O Support for Point 3:
    - O Support for Point 3:

___Write Introduction/Attention-getter

___Write Conclusion/Summary

___Write outline (to hand in)

___Write out Speech

___Read out loud

___Edit

___Reduce to Keywords (on cards)

___Practice in front of someone (get feedback)

   Signature of person: _____

___Revise

___Practice 2X or more

Turn in this sheet and your outline at the beginning of class!

Name: _____   Date:_____

Speech # _____ Speech Assignment (icebreaker, etc.) _____

Title of Speech: _____

Speaker Assignment Sheet

Speakers: Students will present speeches as assigned. Typically, the subject is of the student's choosing, and may reflect a student's beliefs and values. However, all subjects and language used are to be respectful.

Preparation Checklist:

___ Review notes for assignment (icebreaker, organize your speech, Eye Contact, Vocal
___ Variety, Body Language, Research Your Topic, Tell Your Testimony)

___Brainstorming

___Topic/Subject:

___Research, if necessary

___More Brainstorming, if necessary

___Trial Outline

- Main idea:
- Point 1:
    - O Support for Point 1:
    - O Support for Point 1:
- Point 2:
    - O Support for Point 2:
    - O Support for Point 2:
- Point 3 (optional):
    - O Support for Point 3:
    - O Support for Point 3:

___Write Introduction/Attention-getter

___Write Conclusion/Summary

___Write outline (to hand in)

___Write out Speech

___Read out loud

___Edit

___Reduce to Keywords (on cards)

___Practice in front of someone (get feedback)

___Signature of person: _____

___Revise

___Practice 2X or more

Turn in this sheet and your outline at the beginning of class!

Name: _____   Date:_____

Speech # _____ Speech Assignment (icebreaker, etc.) _____

Title of Speech: _____

Speaker Assignment Sheet

Speakers: Students will present speeches as assigned. Typically, the subject is of the student's choosing, and may reflect a student's beliefs and values. However, all subjects and language used are to be respectful.

Preparation Checklist:

___ Review notes for assignment (icebreaker, organize your speech, Eye Contact, Vocal
        Variety, Body Language, Research Your Topic, Tell Your Testimony)
___Brainstorming
___Topic/Subject:
___Research, if necessary
___More Brainstorming, if necessary
___Trial Outline
    • Main idea:
    • Point 1:
            O Support for Point 1:
            O Support for Point 1:
    • Point 2:
            O Support for Point 2:
            O Support for Point 2:
    •Point 3 (optional):
            O Support for Point 3:
            O Support for Point 3:
___Write Introduction/Attention-getter
___Write Conclusion/Summary
___Write outline (to hand in)
___Write out Speech
___Read out loud
___Edit
___Reduce to Keywords (on cards)
___Practice in front of someone (get feedback)
    Signature of person: _____
___Revise
___Practice 2X or more

Turn in this sheet and your outline at the beginning of class!

Name: _____   Date:_____

Speech # _____ Speech Assignment (icebreaker, etc.) _____

Title of Speech: _____

Speaker Assignment Sheet

Speakers: Students will present speeches as assigned. Typically, the subject is of the student's choosing, and may reflect a student's beliefs and values. However, all subjects and language used are to be respectful.

Preparation Checklist:

____ Review notes for assignment (icebreaker, organize your speech, Eye Contact, Vocal
       Variety, Body Language, Research Your Topic, Tell Your Testimony)
___Brainstorming
___Topic/Subject:
___Research, if necessary
___More Brainstorming, if necessary
___Trial Outline
     • Main idea:
     • Point 1:
          O Support for Point 1:
          O Support for Point 1:
     • Point 2:
          O Support for Point 2:
          O Support for Point 2:
     •Point 3 (optional):
          O Support for Point 3:
          O Support for Point 3:
___Write Introduction/Attention-getter
___Write Conclusion/Summary
___Write outline (to hand in)
___Write out Speech
___Read out loud
___Edit
___Reduce to Keywords (on cards)
___Practice in front of someone (get feedback)
    Signature of person: _____
___Revise
___Practice 2X or more

Turn in this sheet and your outline at the beginning of class!

Name: _____   Date:_____

Speech # _____ Speech Assignment (icebreaker, etc.) _____

Title of Speech: _____

Speaker Assignment Sheet

Speakers: Students will present speeches as assigned. Typically, the subject is of the student's choosing, and may reflect a student's beliefs and values. However, all subjects and language used are to be respectful.

Preparation Checklist:

____ Review notes for assignment (icebreaker, organize your speech, Eye Contact, Vocal Variety, Body Language, Research Your Topic, Tell Your Testimony)

___Brainstorming

___Topic/Subject:

___Research, if necessary

___More Brainstorming, if necessary

___Trial Outline

- • Main idea:
- • Point 1:
  - O Support for Point 1:
  - O Support for Point 1:
- • Point 2:
  - O Support for Point 2:
  - O Support for Point 2:
- •Point 3 (optional):
  - O Support for Point 3:
  - O Support for Point 3:

___Write Introduction/Attention-getter

___Write Conclusion/Summary

___Write outline (to hand in)

___Write out Speech

___Read out loud

___Edit

___Reduce to Keywords (on cards)

___Practice in front of someone (get feedback)

Signature of person: _____

___Revise

___Practice 2X or more

Turn in this sheet and your outline at the beginning of class!

Name: _____   Date:_____

Speech # _____ Speech Assignment (icebreaker, etc.) _____

Title of Speech: _____

Speaker Assignment Sheet

Speakers: Students will present speeches as assigned. Typically, the subject is of the student's choosing, and may reflect a student's beliefs and values. However, all subjects and language used are to be respectful.

Preparation Checklist:

___ Review notes for assignment (icebreaker, organize your speech, Eye Contact, Vocal Variety, Body Language, Research Your Topic, Tell Your Testimony)

___Brainstorming

___Topic/Subject:

___Research, if necessary

___More Brainstorming, if necessary

___Trial Outline
- • Main idea:
- • Point 1:
  - O Support for Point 1:
  - O Support for Point 1:
- • Point 2:
  - O Support for Point 2:
  - O Support for Point 2:
- •Point 3 (optional):
  - O Support for Point 3:
  - O Support for Point 3:

___Write Introduction/Attention-getter

___Write Conclusion/Summary

___Write outline (to hand in)

___Write out Speech

___Read out loud

___Edit

___Reduce to Keywords (on cards)

___Practice in front of someone (get feedback)

Signature of person: _____

___Revise

___Practice 2X or more

Turn in this sheet and your outline at the beginning of class!

Name: _____   Date:_____

Speech # _____ Speech Assignment (icebreaker, etc.) _____

Title of Speech: _____

Speaker Assignment Sheet

Speakers: Students will present speeches as assigned. Typically, the subject is of the student's choosing, and may reflect a student's beliefs and values. However, all subjects and language used are to be respectful.

Preparation Checklist:

____ Review notes for assignment (icebreaker, organize your speech, Eye Contact, Vocal
         Variety, Body Language, Research Your Topic, Tell Your Testimony)
____Brainstorming
____Topic/Subject:
____Research, if necessary
____More Brainstorming, if necessary
____Trial Outline
         • Main idea:
         • Point 1:
                  O Support for Point 1:
                  O Support for Point 1:
         • Point 2:
                  O Support for Point 2:
                  O Support for Point 2:
         •Point 3 (optional):
                  O Support for Point 3:
                  O Support for Point 3:
____Write Introduction/Attention-getter
____Write Conclusion/Summary
____Write outline (to hand in)
____Write out Speech
____Read out loud
____Edit
____Reduce to Keywords (on cards)
____Practice in front of someone (get feedback)
         Signature of person: _____
____Revise
____Practice 2X or more
         Turn in this sheet and your outline at the beginning of class!

Name: _____   Date:_____

Speech # _____ Speech Assignment (icebreaker, etc.) _____

Title of Speech: _____

Speaker Assignment Sheet

Speakers: Students will present speeches as assigned. Typically, the subject is of the student's choosing, and may reflect a student's beliefs and values. However, all subjects and language used are to be respectful.

Preparation Checklist:

___ Review notes for assignment (icebreaker, organize your speech, Eye Contact, Vocal
     Variety, Body Language, Research Your Topic, Tell Your Testimony)
___Brainstorming
___Topic/Subject:
___Research, if necessary
___More Brainstorming, if necessary
___Trial Outline
- Main idea:
- Point 1:
  - O Support for Point 1:
  - O Support for Point 1:
- Point 2:
  - O Support for Point 2:
  - O Support for Point 2:
- Point 3 (optional):
  - O Support for Point 3:
  - O Support for Point 3:

___Write Introduction/Attention-getter
___Write Conclusion/Summary
___Write outline (to hand in)
___Write out Speech
___Read out loud
___Edit
___Reduce to Keywords (on cards)
___Practice in front of someone (get feedback)
    Signature of person: _____
___Revise
___Practice 2X or more

Turn in this sheet and your outline at the beginning of class!

Name: _____   Date:_____

Speech # _____ Speech Assignment (icebreaker, etc.) _____

Title of Speech: _____

Speaker Assignment Sheet

Speakers: Students will present speeches as assigned. Typically, the subject is of the student's choosing, and may reflect a student's beliefs and values. However, all subjects and language used are to be respectful.

Preparation Checklist:

____ Review notes for assignment (icebreaker, organize your speech, Eye Contact, Vocal Variety, Body Language, Research Your Topic, Tell Your Testimony)

___Brainstorming

___Topic/Subject:

___Research, if necessary

___More Brainstorming, if necessary

___Trial Outline

- Main idea:
- Point 1:
    - O Support for Point 1:
    - O Support for Point 1:
- Point 2:
    - O Support for Point 2:
    - O Support for Point 2:
- Point 3 (optional):
    - O Support for Point 3:
    - O Support for Point 3:

___Write Introduction/Attention-getter

___Write Conclusion/Summary

___Write outline (to hand in)

___Write out Speech

___Read out loud

___Edit

___Reduce to Keywords (on cards)

___Practice in front of someone (get feedback)

Signature of person: _____

___Revise

___Practice 2X or more

Turn in this sheet and your outline at the beginning of class!

Name: _____ Date:_____

Speech # _____ Speech Assignment (icebreaker, etc.) _____

Title of Speech: _____

Speaker Assignment Sheet

Speakers: Students will present speeches as assigned. Typically, the subject is of the student's choosing, and may reflect a student's beliefs and values. However, all subjects and language used are to be respectful.

Preparation Checklist:

___ Review notes for assignment (icebreaker, organize your speech, Eye Contact, Vocal Variety, Body Language, Research Your Topic, Tell Your Testimony)

___Brainstorming

___Topic/Subject:

___Research, if necessary

___More Brainstorming, if necessary

___Trial Outline

- Main idea:
- Point 1:
    - O Support for Point 1:
    - O Support for Point 1:
- Point 2:
    - O Support for Point 2:
    - O Support for Point 2:
- Point 3 (optional):
    - O Support for Point 3:
    - O Support for Point 3:

___Write Introduction/Attention-getter

___Write Conclusion/Summary

___Write outline (to hand in)

___Write out Speech

___Read out loud

___Edit

___Reduce to Keywords (on cards)

___Practice in front of someone (get feedback)

Signature of person: _____

___Revise

___Practice 2X or more

Turn in this sheet and your outline at the beginning of class!

Name: _____   Date:_____

Speech # _____ Speech Assignment (icebreaker, etc.) _____

Title of Speech: _____

Speaker Assignment Sheet

Speakers: Students will present speeches as assigned. Typically, the subject is of the student's choosing, and may reflect a student's beliefs and values. However, all subjects and language used are to be respectful.

Preparation Checklist:

____ Review notes for assignment (icebreaker, organize your speech, Eye Contact, Vocal
      Variety, Body Language, Research Your Topic, Tell Your Testimony)
___Brainstorming
___Topic/Subject:
___Research, if necessary
___More Brainstorming, if necessary
___Trial Outline
    • Main idea:
    • Point 1:
            O Support for Point 1:
            O Support for Point 1:
    • Point 2:
            O Support for Point 2:
            O Support for Point 2:
    •Point 3 (optional):
            O Support for Point 3:
            O Support for Point 3:
___Write Introduction/Attention-getter
___Write Conclusion/Summary
___Write outline (to hand in)
___Write out Speech
___Read out loud
___Edit
___Reduce to Keywords (on cards)
___Practice in front of someone (get feedback)
      Signature of person: _____
___Revise
___Practice 2X or more

Turn in this sheet and your outline at the beginning of class!

Name: _____ Date:_____

Speech # _____ Speech Assignment (icebreaker, etc.) _____

Title of Speech: _____

Speaker Assignment Sheet

Speakers: Students will present speeches as assigned. Typically, the subject is of the student's choosing, and may reflect a student's beliefs and values. However, all subjects and language used are to be respectful.

Preparation Checklist:

___ Review notes for assignment (icebreaker, organize your speech, Eye Contact, Vocal Variety, Body Language, Research Your Topic, Tell Your Testimony)

___Brainstorming

___Topic/Subject:

___Research, if necessary

___More Brainstorming, if necessary

___Trial Outline

- • Main idea:
- • Point 1:
    - O Support for Point 1:
    - O Support for Point 1:
- • Point 2:
    - O Support for Point 2:
    - O Support for Point 2:
- •Point 3 (optional):
    - O Support for Point 3:
    - O Support for Point 3:

___Write Introduction/Attention-getter

___Write Conclusion/Summary

___Write outline (to hand in)

___Write out Speech

___Read out loud

___Edit

___Reduce to Keywords (on cards)

___Practice in front of someone (get feedback)

___Signature of person: _____

___Revise

___Practice 2X or more

Turn in this sheet and your outline at the beginning of class!

Name: _____   Date:_____

Speech # _____ Speech Assignment (icebreaker, etc.) _____

Title of Speech: _____

Speaker Assignment Sheet

Speakers: Students will present speeches as assigned. Typically, the subject is of the student's choosing, and may reflect a student's beliefs and values. However, all subjects and language used are to be respectful.

Preparation Checklist:

____ Review notes for assignment (icebreaker, organize your speech, Eye Contact, Vocal Variety, Body Language, Research Your Topic, Tell Your Testimony)

____Brainstorming

____Topic/Subject:

____Research, if necessary

____More Brainstorming, if necessary

____Trial Outline

- • Main idea:
- • Point 1:
  - O Support for Point 1:
  - O Support for Point 1:
- • Point 2:
  - O Support for Point 2:
  - O Support for Point 2:
- •Point 3 (optional):
  - O Support for Point 3:
  - O Support for Point 3:

____Write Introduction/Attention-getter

____Write Conclusion/Summary

____Write outline (to hand in)

____Write out Speech

____Read out loud

____Edit

____Reduce to Keywords (on cards)

____Practice in front of someone (get feedback)

Signature of person: _____

____Revise

____Practice 2X or more

Turn in this sheet and your outline at the beginning of class!

Name: _____   Date:_____

Speech # _____ Speech Assignment (icebreaker, etc.) _____

Title of Speech: _____

Speaker Assignment Sheet

Speakers: Students will present speeches as assigned. Typically, the subject is of the student's choosing, and may reflect a student's beliefs and values. However, all subjects and language used are to be respectful.

Preparation Checklist:

____ Review notes for assignment (icebreaker, organize your speech, Eye Contact, Vocal Variety, Body Language, Research Your Topic, Tell Your Testimony)

___Brainstorming

___Topic/Subject:

___Research, if necessary

___More Brainstorming, if necessary

___Trial Outline

- Main idea:
- Point 1:
    - O Support for Point 1:
    - O Support for Point 1:
- Point 2:
    - O Support for Point 2:
    - O Support for Point 2:
- Point 3 (optional):
    - O Support for Point 3:
    - O Support for Point 3:

___Write Introduction/Attention-getter

___Write Conclusion/Summary

___Write outline (to hand in)

___Write out Speech

___Read out loud

___Edit

___Reduce to Keywords (on cards)

___Practice in front of someone (get feedback)

Signature of person: _____

___Revise

___Practice 2X or more

Turn in this sheet and your outline at the beginning of class!

Evaluator Assignment

Evaluator Assignment

Evaluators: No preparation required prior to class. During class, evaluators will listen and watch their assigned speaker carefully, outlining the speech. There will be one minute of silence after each speaker to give the evaluators time to work on their evaluation notes. After all prepared speeches, the evaluators will present their 1-2 minute evaluations in turn. Focus on areas the speaker did well and pick just a couple areas for improvement. Use the sandwich approach!

Outline

Organization   **Evaluation Notes:**

- ✓ Clear beginning, middle, end
- ✓ Opening grabs attention
- ✓ Body
  - ○ A few main points
  - ○ Points supported
- ✓ Good transitions
- ✓ Close—strong (summary, call for action

Delivery

- ✓ Physical appearance
- ✓ Manner (confident, enthusiastic)
- ✓ Vocal variety, Pacing
- ✓ Word choice
- ✓ Eye contact
- ✓ Any distracting mannerisms?
- ✓ Use of gestures
- ✓ Body Language
- ✓ Use of props

Purpose

- ✓ Did the speaker help you care about the topic?
- ✓ Did the speaker keep your attention?
- ✓ Do think differently or want to act differently?

Evaluator Assignment

Evaluators: No preparation required prior to class. During class, evaluators will listen and watch their assigned speaker carefully, outlining the speech. There will be one minute of silence after each speaker to give the evaluators time to work on their evaluation notes. After all prepared speeches, the evaluators will present their 1-2 minute evaluations in turn. Focus on areas the speaker did well and pick just a couple areas for improvement. Use the sandwich approach!

Outline

Organization   **Evaluation Notes:**

- ✓ Clear beginning, middle, end
- ✓ Opening grabs attention
- ✓ Body
    - ○ A few main points
    - ○ Points supported
- ✓ Good transitions
- ✓ Close—strong (summary, call for action

Delivery

- ✓ Physical appearance
- ✓ Manner (confident, enthusiastic)
- ✓ Vocal variety, Pacing
- ✓ Word choice
- ✓ Eye contact
- ✓ Any distracting mannerisms?
- ✓ Use of gestures
- ✓ Body Language
- ✓ Use of props

Purpose

- ✓ Did the speaker help you care about the topic?
- ✓ Did the speaker keep your attention?
- ✓ Do think differently or want to act differently?

Evaluator Assignment

Evaluators: No preparation required prior to class. During class, evaluators will listen and watch their assigned speaker carefully, outlining the speech. There will be one minute of silence after each speaker to give the evaluators time to work on their evaluation notes. After all prepared speeches, the evaluators will present their 1-2 minute evaluations in turn. Focus on areas the speaker did well and pick just a couple areas for improvement. Use the sandwich approach!

Outline

Organization   **Evaluation Notes:**

- ✓ Clear beginning, middle, end
- ✓ Opening grabs attention
- ✓ Body
    - ○ A few main points
    - ○ Points supported
- ✓ Good transitions
- ✓ Close—strong (summary, call for action

Delivery

- ✓ Physical appearance
- ✓ Manner (confident, enthusiastic)
- ✓ Vocal variety, Pacing
- ✓ Word choice
- ✓ Eye contact
- ✓ Any distracting mannerisms?
- ✓ Use of gestures
- ✓ Body Language
- ✓ Use of props

Purpose

- ✓ Did the speaker help you care about the topic?
- ✓ Did the speaker keep your attention?
- ✓ Do think differently or want to act differently?

Evaluator Assignment

Evaluators: No preparation required prior to class. During class, evaluators will listen and watch their assigned speaker carefully, outlining the speech. There will be one minute of silence after each speaker to give the evaluators time to work on their evaluation notes. After all prepared speeches, the evaluators will present their 1-2 minute evaluations in turn. Focus on areas the speaker did well and pick just a couple areas for improvement. Use the sandwich approach!

Outline

Organization

✓ Clear beginning, middle, end
✓ Opening grabs attention
✓ Body
  o A few main points
  o Points supported
✓ Good transitions
✓ Close—strong (summary, call for action

Delivery

✓ Physical appearance
✓ Manner (confident, enthusiastic)
✓ Vocal variety, Pacing
✓ Word choice
✓ Eye contact
✓ Any distracting mannerisms?
✓ Use of gestures
✓ Body Language
✓ Use of props

Purpose

✓ Did the speaker help you care about the topic?
✓ Did the speaker keep your attention?
✓ Do think differently or want to act differently?

Evaluation Notes:

Evaluator Assignment

Evaluators: No preparation required prior to class. During class, evaluators will listen and watch their assigned speaker carefully, outlining the speech. There will be one minute of silence after each speaker to give the evaluators time to work on their evaluation notes. After all prepared speeches, the evaluators will present their 1-2 minute evaluations in turn. Focus on areas the speaker did well and pick just a couple areas for improvement. Use the sandwich approach!

Outline

Organization

- ✓ Clear beginning, middle, end
- ✓ Opening grabs attention
- ✓ Body
    - ○ A few main points
    - ○ Points supported
- ✓ Good transitions
- ✓ Close—strong (summary, call for action

Delivery

- ✓ Physical appearance
- ✓ Manner (confident, enthusiastic)
- ✓ Vocal variety, Pacing
- ✓ Word choice
- ✓ Eye contact
- ✓ Any distracting mannerisms?
- ✓ Use of gestures
- ✓ Body Language
- ✓ Use of props

Purpose

- ✓ Did the speaker help you care about the topic?
- ✓ Did the speaker keep your attention?
- ✓ Do think differently or want to act differently?

Evaluation Notes:

Evaluator Assignment

Evaluators: No preparation required prior to class. During class, evaluators will listen and watch their assigned speaker carefully, outlining the speech. There will be one minute of silence after each speaker to give the evaluators time to work on their evaluation notes. After all prepared speeches, the evaluators will present their 1-2 minute evaluations in turn. Focus on areas the speaker did well and pick just a couple areas for improvement. Use the sandwich approach!

Outline

Organization   **Evaluation Notes:**

- ✓ Clear beginning, middle, end
- ✓ Opening grabs attention
- ✓ Body
    - ○ A few main points
    - ○ Points supported
- ✓ Good transitions
- ✓ Close—strong (summary, call for action

Delivery

- ✓ Physical appearance
- ✓ Manner (confident, enthusiastic)
- ✓ Vocal variety, Pacing
- ✓ Word choice
- ✓ Eye contact
- ✓ Any distracting mannerisms?
- ✓ Use of gestures
- ✓ Body Language
- ✓ Use of props

Purpose

- ✓ Did the speaker help you care about the topic?
- ✓ Did the speaker keep your attention?
- ✓ Do think differently or want to act differently?

Evaluator Assignment

Evaluators: No preparation required prior to class. During class, evaluators will listen and watch their assigned speaker carefully, outlining the speech. There will be one minute of silence after each speaker to give the evaluators time to work on their evaluation notes. After all prepared speeches, the evaluators will present their 1-2 minute evaluations in turn. Focus on areas the speaker did well and pick just a couple areas for improvement. Use the sandwich approach!

Outline

Organization   **Evaluation Notes:**

- ✓ Clear beginning, middle, end
- ✓ Opening grabs attention
- ✓ Body
    - ○ A few main points
    - ○ Points supported
- ✓ Good transitions
- ✓ Close—strong (summary, call for action

Delivery

- ✓ Physical appearance
- ✓ Manner (confident, enthusiastic)
- ✓ Vocal variety, Pacing
- ✓ Word choice
- ✓ Eye contact
- ✓ Any distracting mannerisms?
- ✓ Use of gestures
- ✓ Body Language
- ✓ Use of props

Purpose

- ✓ Did the speaker help you care about the topic?
- ✓ Did the speaker keep your attention?
- ✓ Do think differently or want to act differently?

Evaluator Assignment

Evaluators: No preparation required prior to class. During class, evaluators will listen and watch their assigned speaker carefully, outlining the speech. There will be one minute of silence after each speaker to give the evaluators time to work on their evaluation notes. After all prepared speeches, the evaluators will present their 1-2 minute evaluations in turn. Focus on areas the speaker did well and pick just a couple areas for improvement. Use the sandwich approach!

Outline

Organization

- ✓ Clear beginning, middle, end
- ✓ Opening grabs attention
- ✓ Body
    - ○ A few main points
    - ○ Points supported
- ✓ Good transitions
- ✓ Close—strong (summary, call for action

Delivery

- ✓ Physical appearance
- ✓ Manner (confident, enthusiastic)
- ✓ Vocal variety, Pacing
- ✓ Word choice
- ✓ Eye contact
- ✓ Any distracting mannerisms?
- ✓ Use of gestures
- ✓ Body Language
- ✓ Use of props

Purpose

- ✓ Did the speaker help you care about the topic?
- ✓ Did the speaker keep your attention?
- ✓ Do think differently or want to act differently?

Evaluation Notes:

Evaluator Assignment

Evaluators: No preparation required prior to class. During class, evaluators will listen and watch their assigned speaker carefully, outlining the speech. There will be one minute of silence after each speaker to give the evaluators time to work on their evaluation notes. After all prepared speeches, the evaluators will present their 1-2 minute evaluations in turn. Focus on areas the speaker did well and pick just a couple areas for improvement. Use the sandwich approach!

Outline	Organization	Evaluation Notes:

Organization

- ✓ Clear beginning, middle, end
- ✓ Opening grabs attention
- ✓ Body
    - o A few main points
    - o Points supported
- ✓ Good transitions
- ✓ Close—strong (summary, call for action

Delivery

- ✓ Physical appearance
- ✓ Manner (confident, enthusiastic)
- ✓ Vocal variety, Pacing
- ✓ Word choice
- ✓ Eye contact
- ✓ Any distracting mannerisms?
- ✓ Use of gestures
- ✓ Body Language
- ✓ Use of props

Purpose

- ✓ Did the speaker help you care about the topic?
- ✓ Did the speaker keep your attention?
- ✓ Do think differently or want to act differently?

Impromptu Leader Assignment

Impromptu Leader Assignment

Impromptu Leader*: Prior to class, the Impromptu Leader will do 3 things: select a theme, prepare questions related to the theme and prepare a 1-2 minute talk to introduce the theme. During class, after introducing the theme, the Impromptu Leader will state a question and then call randomly on impromptu participants to respond for 1-2 minutes. Each impromptu participant should have a different question.

Theme:

1-2 minute talk to introduce theme (Key points):

Typically call on the people who are NOT: giving a speech, timer, evaluator or grammarian

# of Questions needed = _____

List of Questions:

Impromptu Leader Assignment

Impromptu Leader*: Prior to class, the Impromptu Leader will do 3 things: select a theme, prepare questions related to the theme and prepare a 1-2 minute talk to introduce the theme. During class, after introducing the theme, the Impromptu Leader will state a question and then call randomly on impromptu participants to respond for 1-2 minutes. Each impromptu participant should have a different question.

Theme:

1-2 minute talk to introduce theme (Key points):

Typically call on the people who are NOT: giving a speech, timer, evaluator or grammarian

# of Questions needed = _____

List of Questions:

Impromptu Leader Assignment

Impromptu Leader*: Prior to class, the Impromptu Leader will do 3 things: select a theme, prepare questions related to the theme and prepare a 1-2 minute talk to introduce the theme. During class, after introducing the theme, the Impromptu Leader will state a question and then call randomly on impromptu participants to respond for 1-2 minutes. Each impromptu participant should have a different question.

Theme:

1-2 minute talk to introduce theme (Key points):

Typically call on the people who are NOT: giving a speech, timer, evaluator or grammarian

# of Questions needed = _____

List of Questions:

Impromptu Leader Assignment

Impromptu Leader*: Prior to class, the Impromptu Leader will do 3 things: select a theme, prepare questions related to the theme and prepare a 1-2 minute talk to introduce the theme. During class, after introducing the theme, the Impromptu Leader will state a question and then call randomly on impromptu participants to respond for 1-2 minutes.   Each impromptu participant should have a different question.

Theme:

1-2 minute talk to introduce theme (Key points):

Typically call on the people who are NOT: giving a speech, timer, evaluator or grammarian

# of Questions needed = _____

 List of Questions:

Impromptu Leader Assignment

Impromptu Leader*: Prior to class, the Impromptu Leader will do 3 things: select a theme, prepare questions related to the theme and prepare a 1-2 minute talk to introduce the theme. During class, after introducing the theme, the Impromptu Leader will state a question and then call randomly on impromptu participants to respond for 1-2 minutes.   Each impromptu participant should have a different question.

Theme:

1-2 minute talk to introduce theme (Key points):

Typically call on the people who are NOT: giving a speech, timer, evaluator or grammarian

# of Questions needed = _____

 List of Questions:

Impromptu Leader Assignment

Impromptu Leader*: Prior to class, the Impromptu Leader will do 3 things: select a theme, prepare questions related to the theme and prepare a 1-2 minute talk to introduce the theme. During class, after introducing the theme, the Impromptu Leader will state a question and then call randomly on impromptu participants to respond for 1-2 minutes. Each impromptu participant should have a different question.

Theme:

1-2 minute talk to introduce theme (Key points):

Typically call on the people who are NOT: giving a speech, timer, evaluator or grammarian

# of Questions needed = _____

 List of Questions:

Grammarian Assignment

Grammarian Assignment Sheet

Grammarian: Prior to class, the grammarian picks a word of the day for people to try to use in their presentations. The grammarian should prepare by writing out 3 things: 1. the word of the day written in large letters on a paper (which will be placed so that speakers can see it during class), 2. the definition (to read aloud during class) and 3. an original sample sentence or two, also to be read in class.

Word of the day:

> **Definition**

> **1-2 original sample sentences using the word of the day**

Word of the Day

Bring the Word of the Day written in large letters on an 8.5X11" sheet of paper

Name	Word of the Day Day used	Ah, Er, Um, You Know	Colorful uses of the English language

During class, tally each student's use of the word of the day and also tally "filler" words

Grammarian Assignment Sheet

Grammarian: Prior to class, the grammarian picks a word of the day for people to try to use in their presentations. The grammarian should prepare by writing out 3 things: 1. the word of the day written in large letters on a paper (which will be placed so that speakers can see it during class), 2. the definition (to read aloud during class) and 3. an original sample sentence or two, also to be read in class.

Word of the day:

   Definition

   1-2 original sample sentences using the word of the day

Word of the Day

Bring the Word of the Day written in large letters on an 8.5X11" sheet of paper

Name	Word of the Day used	Ah, Er, Um, You Know	Colorful uses of the English language

During class, tally each student's use of the word of the day and also tally "filler" words

Grammarian Assignment Sheet

Grammarian: Prior to class, the grammarian picks a word of the day for people to try to use in their presentations. The grammarian should prepare by writing out 3 things: 1. the word of the day written in large letters on a paper (which will be placed so that speakers can see it during class), 2. the definition (to read aloud during class) and 3. an original sample sentence or two, also to be read in class.

Word of the day:

    Definition

```
┌──────────────────────────────┐
│                              │
│      Word of the Day         │
│                              │
│                              │
└──────────────────────────────┘
```

    1-2 original sample sentences using the word of the day

Bring the Word of the Day written in large letters on an 8.5X11" sheet of paper

Name	Word of the Day used	Ah, Er, Um, You Know	Colorful uses of the English language

During class, tally each student's use of the word of the day and also tally "filler" words

Grammarian Assignment Sheet

Grammarian: Prior to class, the grammarian picks a word of the day for people to try to use in their presentations. The grammarian should prepare by writing out 3 things: 1. the word of the day written in large letters on a paper (which will be placed so that speakers can see it during class), 2. the definition (to read aloud during class) and 3. an original sample sentence or two, also to be read in class.

Word of the day:

   Definition

   1-2 original sample sentences using the word of the day

Word of the Day

Bring the Word of the Day written in large letters on an 8.5X11" sheet of paper

Name	Word of the Day used	Ah, Er, Um, You Know	Colorful uses of the English language

During class, tally each student's use of the word of the day and also tally "filler" words

Grammarian Assignment Sheet

Grammarian: Prior to class, the grammarian picks a word of the day for people to try to use in their presentations. The grammarian should prepare by writing out 3 things: 1. the word of the day written in large letters on a paper (which will be placed so that speakers can see it during class), 2. the definition (to read aloud during class) and 3. an original sample sentence or two, also to be read in class.

Word of the day:

Definition

1-2 original sample sentences using the word of the day

Word of the Day

Bring the Word of the Day written in large letters on an 8.5X11" sheet of paper

Name	Word of the Day used	Ah, Er, Um, You Know	Colorful uses of the English language

During class, tally each student's use of the word of the day and also tally "filler" words

Grammarian Assignment Sheet

Grammarian: Prior to class, the grammarian picks a word of the day for people to try to use in their presentations. The grammarian should prepare by writing out 3 things: 1. the word of the day written in large letters on a paper (which will be placed so that speakers can see it during class), 2. the definition (to read aloud during class) and 3. an original sample sentence or two, also to be read in class.

Word of the day:

   Definition

   1-2 original sample sentences using the word of the day

Word of the Day

Bring the Word of the Day written in large letters on an 8.5X11" sheet of paper

Name	Word of the	Ah, Er, Um, You Know	Colorful uses of the English language

During class, tally each student's use of the word of the day and also tally "filler" words

Timer Assignment

Timer: No preparation required prior to class. During class the timer will time the following using a stop watch or other device: prepared speeches, evaluations and impromptu participants. During each of the timed presentations, the timer will hold up green, yellow and red folders to give the speaker an indication of their time.

At the start of class, obtain timing device, timing cards and confirm times.

Duty	Name	Time
Speaker 1		
Speaker 2		
Speaker 3		
Speaker 4		
Speaker 5		
Speaker 6		
Speaker 7		
Speaker 8		
Speaker 9		
Speaker 10		
Evaluator 1		
Evaluator 2		
Evaluator 3		
Evaluator 4		
Evaluator 5		
Evaluator 6		
Evaluator 7		
Evaluator 8		
Evaluator 9		
Evaluator 10		
Impromptu 1		
Impromptu 2		
Impromptu 3		
Impromptu 4		
Impromptu 5		
Impromptu 6		
Impromptu 7		

Prepared Speeches
Min time (green): _____
Mid time (yellow): _____
Max time (red): _____
Ex. 3/4/5 or 5/6/7 minutes

Evaluations
Min time (green): _____
Mid time (yellow): _____
Max time (red): _____
Ex. 45/60/1:15 or 1/1:30/2 min

Impromptu Speaking
Min time (green): _____
Mid time (yellow): _____
Max time (red): _____
Ex. 30/45/60 sec or 1/1:30/2 min

Timer Assignment Sheet

Timer: No preparation required prior to class. During class the timer will time the following using a stop watch or other device: prepared speeches, evaluations and impromptu participants. During each of the timed presentations, the timer will hold up green, yellow and red folders to give the speaker an indication of their time.

At the start of class, obtain timing device, timing cards and confirm times.

Duty	Name	Time
Speaker 1		
Speaker 2		
Speaker 3		
Speaker 4		
Speaker 5		
Speaker 6		
Speaker 7		
Speaker 8		
Speaker 9		
Speaker 10		
Evaluator 1		
Evaluator 2		
Evaluator 3		
Evaluator 4		
Evaluator 5		
Evaluator 6		
Evaluator 7		
Evaluator 8		
Evaluator 9		
Evaluator 10		
Impromptu 1		
Impromptu 2		
Impromptu 3		
Impromptu 4		
Impromptu 5		
Impromptu 6		
Impromptu 7		

Prepared Speeches
Min time (green): _____
Mid time (yellow): _____
Max time (red): _____
Ex. 3/4/5 or 5/6/7 minutes

Evaluations
Min time (green): _____
Mid time (yellow): _____
Max time (red): _____
Ex. 45/60/1:15 or 1/1:30/2 min

Impromptu Speaking
Min time (green): _____
Mid time (yellow): _____
Max time (red): _____
Ex. 30/45/60 sec or 1/1:30/2 min

Timer Assignment Sheet

Timer: No preparation required prior to class. During class the timer will time the following using a stop watch or other device: prepared speeches, evaluations and impromptu participants. During each of the timed presentations, the timer will hold up green, yellow and red folders to give the speaker an indication of their time.

At the start of class, obtain timing device, timing cards and confirm times.

Duty	Name	Time
Speaker 1		
Speaker 2		
Speaker 3		
Speaker 4		
Speaker 5		
Speaker 6		
Speaker 7		
Speaker 8		
Speaker 9		
Speaker 10		
Evaluator 1		
Evaluator 2		
Evaluator 3		
Evaluator 4		
Evaluator 5		
Evaluator 6		
Evaluator 7		
Evaluator 8		
Evaluator 9		
Evaluator 10		
Impromptu 1		
Impromptu 2		
Impromptu 3		
Impromptu 4		
Impromptu 5		
Impromptu 6		
Impromptu 7		

Prepared Speeches
Min time (green): _____
Mid time (yellow): _____
Max time (red): _____
Ex. 3/4/5 or 5/6/7 minutes

Evaluations
Min time (green): _____
Mid time (yellow): _____
Max time (red): _____
Ex. 45/60/1:15 or 1/1:30/2 min

Impromptu Speaking
Min time (green): _____
Mid time (yellow): _____
Max time (red): _____
Ex. 30/45/60 sec or 1/1:30/2 min

Timer Assignment Sheet

Timer: No preparation required prior to class. During class the timer will time the following using a stop watch or other device: prepared speeches, evaluations and impromptu participants. During each of the timed presentations, the timer will hold up green, yellow and red folders to give the speaker an indication of their time.

At the start of class, obtain timing device, timing cards and confirm times.

Duty	Name	Time
Speaker 1		
Speaker 2		
Speaker 3		
Speaker 4		
Speaker 5		
Speaker 6		
Speaker 7		
Speaker 8		
Speaker 9		
Speaker 10		
Evaluator 1		
Evaluator 2		
Evaluator 3		
Evaluator 4		
Evaluator 5		
Evaluator 6		
Evaluator 7		
Evaluator 8		
Evaluator 9		
Evaluator 10		
Impromptu 1		
Impromptu 2		
Impromptu 3		
Impromptu 4		
Impromptu 5		
Impromptu 6		
Impromptu 7		

Prepared Speeches

Min time (green): _____

Mid time (yellow): _____

Max time (red): _____

Ex. 3/4/5 or 5/6/7 minutes

Evaluations

Min time (green): _____

Mid time (yellow): _____

Max time (red): _____

Ex. 45/60/1:15 or 1/1:30/2 min

Impromptu Speaking

Min time (green): _____

Mid time (yellow): _____

Max time (red): _____

Ex. 30/45/60 sec or 1/1:30/2 min

Timer Assignment Sheet

Timer: No preparation required prior to class. During class the timer will time the following using a stop watch or other device: prepared speeches, evaluations and impromptu participants. During each of the timed presentations, the timer will hold up green, yellow and red folders to give the speaker an indication of their time.

At the start of class, obtain timing device, timing cards and confirm times.

Duty	Name	Time
Speaker 1		
Speaker 2		
Speaker 3		
Speaker 4		
Speaker 5		
Speaker 6		
Speaker 7		
Speaker 8		
Speaker 9		
Speaker 10		
Evaluator 1		
Evaluator 2		
Evaluator 3		
Evaluator 4		
Evaluator 5		
Evaluator 6		
Evaluator 7		
Evaluator 8		
Evaluator 9		
Evaluator 10		
Impromptu 1		
Impromptu 2		
Impromptu 3		
Impromptu 4		
Impromptu 5		
Impromptu 6		
Impromptu 7		

Prepared Speeches
Min time (green): _____
Mid time (yellow): _____
Max time (red): _____
Ex. 3/4/5 or 5/6/7 minutes

Evaluations
Min time (green): _____
Mid time (yellow): _____
Max time (red): _____
Ex. 45/60/1:15 or 1/1:30/2 min

Impromptu Speaking
Min time (green): _____
Mid time (yellow): _____
Max time (red): _____
Ex. 30/45/60 sec or 1/1:30/2 min

Timer Assignment Sheet

Timer: No preparation required prior to class. During class the timer will time the following using a stop watch or other device: prepared speeches, evaluations and impromptu participants. During each of the timed presentations, the timer will hold up green, yellow and red folders to give the speaker an indication of their time.

At the start of class, obtain timing device, timing cards and confirm times.

Duty	Name	Time
Speaker 1		
Speaker 2		
Speaker 3		
Speaker 4		
Speaker 5		
Speaker 6		
Speaker 7		
Speaker 8		
Speaker 9		
Speaker 10		
Evaluator 1		
Evaluator 2		
Evaluator 3		
Evaluator 4		
Evaluator 5		
Evaluator 6		
Evaluator 7		
Evaluator 8		
Evaluator 9		
Evaluator 10		
Impromptu 1		
Impromptu 2		
Impromptu 3		
Impromptu 4		
Impromptu 5		
Impromptu 6		
Impromptu 7		

Prepared Speeches
Min time (green): _____
Mid time (yellow): _____
Max time (red): _____
Ex. 3/4/5 or 5/6/7 minutes

Evaluations
Min time (green): _____
Mid time (yellow): _____
Max time (red): _____
Ex. 45/60/1:15 or 1/1:30/2 min

Impromptu Speaking
Min time (green): _____
Mid time (yellow): _____
Max time (red): _____
Ex. 30/45/60 sec or 1/1:30/2 min

Appendix 5: Assignment Schedules

Sample

Class	1	2	3	4	5	6	7	8	9	10	11	12	13	14	15
Date	9/7	9/14	9/21	9/28	10/5	10/12	10/19	10/26	11/2	11/9	11/16	11/23	11/30	12/7	12/14
Lesson	Overv.	Eval.	Organ.	Intro/c	Eye c.	Vocal	Body L	Stories	Rsrch	Influen	Conflic	Humor	Testim	Skits	Improv
Speech	none	#1	#1	#2	#2	#3	#3	#4	#4	#5	#5	#6	#6	#7	#7
Students															
1. Buddy		#1	IL/EV4	#2	T/EV6	#3	T/EV5	#4	G/EV6	#5	IL/EV5	#6	EV6	#7	IL
2. Hunter		#1	G/EV5	#2	IL/EV4	X	X	#3	#4	#5	T/EV4	#6	G	#7	T/EV6
3. David		#1	T/EV6	#2	G/EV7	#3	IL/EV4	#4	T/EV5	#5	G	#6	IL/EV4	#7	EV5
4. William		IL/EV1	#1	EV3	#2	G/EV7	#3	IL/EV1	#4	T/EV7	#5	G/EV2	#6	IL/EV1	#7
5. Tyler		G/EV2	#1	IL/EV1	#2	T/EV3	#3	G/EV7	#4	IL/EV1	#5	T/EV3	#6	G/EV7	#7
6. Thomas		T/EV3	#1	G/EV2	#2	IL/EV1	#3	T/EV3	#4	G/EV2	#5	IL/EV7	#6	T/EV3	#7
7. Ben		X	#1	T	#2	#3	G/EV6	#4	IL/EV2	#5	EV6	#6	T/EV5	#7	G/EV4
Mrs. W.			EV7		EV5			EV2	EV4	EV3		EV1		EV2	

Speech #1 The Icebreaker
Speech #2 Organize Your Speech
Speech #3 Eye Contact
Speech #4 Vocal Variety
Speech #5 Body Language
Speech #6 Research Your Topic
Speech #7 Tell Your Testimony

EV = Evaluator

IL = Impromptu Leader (call on non-speakers first)

G = Grammarian

T = Timer

X = Student gone

Example:

IL/EV5 means that you are both the Impromptu Leader AND an Evaluator.

You will be evaluating student #5

Semester 1 Fill-in-the-blanks

Available online: http://bit.ly/speechclass1

Class	1	2	3	4	5	6	7	8	9	10	11	12	13	14	15 Note:
Date															
Lesson	Overv.	Eval.	Organ.	Intro/c	Eye c.	Vocal	Body L	Stories	Rsrch	Influen	Conflic	Humor	Testim	Skits	Improv
Speech	none	#1	#1	#2	#2	#3	#3	#4	#4	#5	#5	#6	#6	#7	#7
Students															
1															
2															
3															
4															
5															
6															
7															
8															
9															
10															
11															
12															
13															
14															
15															
16															
17															
18															
19															
20															

EV= Evaluator
IL= Impromptu Leader
G = Grammarian
T = Timer
X = Student Gone
Example: IL/EV5 means that you are both the Impromptu Leader and an Evaluator (of speaker #...

Speech 1 The Icebreaker
Speech 2 Organize Your Speech
Speech 3 Eye Contact
Speech 4 Vocal Variety
Speech 5 Body Language
Speech 6 Research Your Topic
Speech 7 Tell Your Testimony

Semester 2 Fill-in-the-blanks

Available online: http://bit.ly/speechclass2

Class	16	17	18	19	20	21	22	23	24	25	26	27	28	29	30 Note:
Date															
Lesson	Rhet.	Interp.	Dialog.	Intro.	Hist.	Struc.	Etiq.	Brnst	Prob	Panel	Sell	Job	Debate	Debate	Debate
Speech	none	#8	#8	#9	#9	#10	#10	#11	#11	#12	#12	#13	#13	#14	#14
Students															
1															
2															
3															
4															
5															
6															
7															
8															
9															
10															
11															
12															
13															
14															
15															
16															
17															
18															
19															
20															

Speech 8   Rhetorical Devices

Speech 9   Interpretive Reading + intro

Speech 10   Story with Dialogue

Speech 11   Memorized Historical Speech

Speech 12   Structure/Problem

Speech 13   Sell a Product

Speech 14   Debate (use speech #12)

EV= Evaluator

IL= Impromptu Leader

G = Grammarian

T = Timer

X = Student Gone

Example: IL/EV5 means that you are both the Impromptu Leader and an Evaluator (of speaker #

Blank assignment sheet

Available online: http://bit.ly/speechclassblank

Class								Note:
Date								
Lesson								
Speech								
Students								
1								
2								
3								
4								
5								
6								
7								
8								
9								
10								
11								
12								
13								
14								
15								
16								
17								
18								
19								
20								

Speech #_
Speech #_
Speech #_
Speech #_
Speech #_
Speech #_
Speech #_

EV= Evaluator
IL= Impromptu Leader
G = Grammarian
T = Timer
X = Student Gone
Example: IL/EV5 means that you are both the Impromptu Leader and an Evaluator (of speaker #

Made in the USA
Lexington, KY
18 August 2019